MACARONI & CHEESE

by Marlena Spieler

MACARONI & CHEESE

PHOTOGRAPHS BY NOEL BARNHURST

CHRONICLE BOOKS

SAN FRANCISCO

Text copyright © 2006 by **Marlena Spieler.**
Photographs copyright © 2006 by **Noel Barnhurst.**

Library of Congress Cataloging-in-Publication Data available.

ISBN 978-0-8118-4962-3

Manufactured in China

Designed by **Jay Peter Salvas**
This book was typeset in **Agenda 9/12** and **Eldorado 9.5/12.25**
Typesetting by **Janis Reed**
Food styling by **Sandra Cook**
Food Stylist's Assistants: **Penny Zweidinger** and
    Elisabet Dernederlanden
Photograher's assistants: **Sara Johnson Loehmann,**
    Gene Lee, and **June Young Lim**

10 9 8 7 6 5

Chronicle Books LLC
680 Second Street
San Francisco, California 94107

www.chroniclebooks.com

To **Leah, Gretchen, Jon, and Alan,**
with love and macaroni . . .
and oodles of melty cheese.

ACKNOWLEDGMENTS

Marlena would like to thank:

Her mom, Caroline Smith, and aunt, Estelle Opper, for *lokshen* and cheese suppers throughout her childhood.

Thanks to Leah, whose childhood was happy as long as Leah's Homey Greek Macaroni and Cheese (page 65) was on the horizon, and to her husband, Jon, for being a great Webmaster as well as a macaroni and cheese devotee. To Gretchen, who perks her nose up fetchingly when there is a possibility of macaroni and cheese.

To Sandy Waks for sharing sheep's milk cheese, especially feta, at our special *zaatar* and flatbread breakfasts; Kamala for just being Kamala; Paula Aspin *et sa famille* for sharing cheese adventures; Judy Reay for tales of macaroni pie in Trinidad; Eileen Adams for macaroni and cheese dreams; Kiwi McLaughlan; Ben Windsor and Jenny Linford; cousin Melissa Opper, who, along with her brother Steven, charmed the good people of Paris; and to cousin Matthew Carl, who joined in with gusto on our cheese plate adventure in New York City.

To Clark Wolf, whose passion and knowledge of cheese is vast and generous, and who always makes me laugh, and to Patricia Schneider for enthusiasm and generosity, as well as very good ideas. To the cheese makers devoted to their craft—Cowgirl Creamery, Point Reyes Blue, Andante, Laurel Chenel, the mozzarella makers of Campania, and every cheese maker who has ever welcomed me into a steamy, milky, fragrant cheese room. To Darryl Corti, wine expert and purveyor of amazing delicacies.

I'm "Emmenthally grateful" to Anne Dettmer and her company, Artisannes, for the fabulous cheeses of Switzerland, and to Randall Hodgson of Neal's Yard Dairy for cheese excellence. To Silvija Davidson of Slow Food and the Oxford Symposium on Food and Cookery for her good taste always; Wendy Fogarty, whose dedication to Slow Food International is inspiring; Jenni Muir, whose hard work and sound judgment are always appreciated. To Sheona and Antonio Vianello, even if Tony can't stand cheese!

To Sotiris Kitrilakis of Zante Feast and Mount Vikos Cheese for teaching me almost everything there is to know about Greek cheese, and to his wife, Rochelle Jolley, just for being wonderful. For support and information, thanks to Marie Jose Sevilla, London's Spanish Trade Commission, and my dear friend Antonietta Stefanic and London's Italian Trade Commission.

Thanks to the late Pietro Pesce and to Maureen Pesce of DanMar International for pecorino delights (as well as truffled lard to make me swoon), to Elaine and David Ashton of Grania and Sarnia Importers, and Allen Laidlow of *The New York Times* commissary for the secrets of macaroni pie.

Thanks to Michele Lomuto and Manuela Barzan, of the Naples, Italy, Chamber of Commerce, who have been so helpful to me in my explorations of the artisanal cheeses and pastas of Campagnia and the joys of mozzarella di bufala.

Thanks to the entire country of France for being an endless source of superb cheeses, and to Italy for the pasta, 750 types at least.

To the *San Francisco Chronicle* food page editors par excellence Michael Bauer and Miriam Morgan, who not only come up with great ideas but also laugh at my jokes. Thank you for sending me on a Roving Feast. To fellow cheese adventuress Kim Severson of *The New York Times* and to the rest of my wonderful, cheese-loving colleagues.

To www.egullet.org, for always being there whenever I needed them, any time of the day or night, anywhere in the world.

To Portia Smith for her invaluable assistance, and to Alan for asking, whenever we neared mealtime during the recipe testing for this book, "What's for macaroni and cheese today?"

To Frank D'Alessandro of International Marketing for a wonderful lunch in Campania, Edouard Cointreau and his marvellous World Gourmand Events, and Saara Rimon of Finnfacts; Rose Levy Beranbaum, Fran McCullough, and Alexandra Sofis, all of whom love mac and cheese. Oscar Leonessa and his family business Leonessa Pasta, which makes divine artisanal pasta, Napoli style; Caroline Campion for her love of baba; and Oscar Bencivenga, without whom we would be lost in Benevento. To the indefatigable Flavia, who always remains cool and cheerful no matter what the challenge, and her Luca, who is as cheerful as she is.

To the California Milk Advisory Board and the American Cheese Society.

To Bee Wilson, who is as delightful to read as she is to spend time with.

To Noel Barnhurst for making the beautiful-tasting mac and cheese look picture-perfect gorgeous.

To Bill LeBlond for saying Yes! when I asked. To Deborah Kops, kind and careful editor, and to Amy Treadwell, who once again led me from page one to the end of a joy-to-cook-and-create project.

And to Madeleine for being the best pussycat and proofreader I could ask for.

Table Of Contents

INTRODUCTION

"Life is half magic, and half pasta."—Federico Fellini

Who can resist macaroni and cheese? Not me! It's a divine accompaniment to any meat or poultry—think of macaroni and crusty Cheddar next to spicy, smoky, or curried sausages, or pasta and fragrant Emmenthal with chicken and mushrooms—or on its own as a robust vegetarian course to delight even the most committed carnivore.

Macaroni and cheese calls to me when I enter my kitchen tired from a long day, and I'm hungry, and everyone around me is hungry, and I can't even think clearly to organize a meal. I put the water on to boil and look around the refrigerator for cheeses that look ready to grate and toss into my hot pasta. Maybe they are very interesting—a chunk of strong Cheddar; a wedge of pungent blue; a slab of fragrant, cave-aged Gruyère. If I'm lucky I have some crème fraîche, or the energy to make a little béchamel. Immediately, I'm in a happy frame of mind, awaiting my macaroni and cheese dinner, the coziest bowlful I know. If I were a cat, I'd be purring at this point.

Those who love macaroni and cheese probably loved it as children, too. Do you remember the casserole of chewy macaroni, topped with crispy crumbs and awash in rich, saucy cheese, spooned up lovingly from a big pan at home, or ladled onto your tray at the school cafeteria? Was mac and cheese the only thing that could brighten days when boring teachers droned on and on and you thought you'd never grow up? While I loved the traditional casserole that we ate at school, at home we ate a different sort of macaroni and cheese—*lokshen* (Yiddish for "noodles"), buttered and tossed with cottage cheese. I would have eaten it every night if I had been allowed to! Even today, there are times when that is my choice of supper, lunch, or midnight snack for more days in a row than I might want to admit!

As a grown-up I have discovered that macaroni and cheese can be even better than that of childhood. For one thing, the adult me usually adds a chopped clove of garlic to my revered *lokshen* and cheese. And instead of confining myself to mac and cheese the all-American way, I've gone global, with spunky artisanal regional American cheeses or luscious traditional European ones, pungent herbs, spiky salsas, a whiff of truffle, and a splash of extra-virgin. Suddenly, my childhood favorite has become a smorgasbord of possibilities!

Macaroni and cheese is an American culinary icon: a simple but perfect dish of pasta and melted cheese, traditionally prepared with a bit of something creamy such as béchamel to hold it together. This dish, in fact, originated on the other side of "the Pond" and has a venerable history stretching back in England to the court of Richard II, where it was a great favorite.

The first written recipe seems to be from *The Experienced English Housekeeper*, by a Mrs. Elizabeth Raffald. Published in 1769, it appears to be the forerunner of our own American classic: béchamel sauce with Cheddar, mixed with macaroni, sprinkled with Parmesan, then baked until bubbly and golden. Another recipe, *macaroni à la reine* ("macaroni in the style of the queen"), made from a similar mixture of pasta, cream, and melty cheese (often Gruyère), appeared frequently in British cookery books until relatively recent times.

Though I'm sure that the early settlers made something similar, macaroni and cheese as a concept was enthusiastically placed on the American table by Thomas Jefferson, the third president of the United States. When he lived in Paris as a diplomat (treaty commissioner to France), he brought his chef slave, James Hemmings, with him to attend cooking school. When he returned home, he wanted his meals to reflect the delicious things he ate in Europe during his four-year sojourn. One of the dishes that Jefferson was taken with was macaroni and cheese. To replicate it at home, he imported a pasta rolling machine and a large amount of Parmesan cheese from Italy. Macaroni and cheese was soon a favorite dish at his Monticello home, and when Jefferson arrived at the White House, he put macaroni and cheese right on the menu.

Mac and cheese became an intrinsic part of American cookery, taking on different flavorings, depending on the region and the ethnic group preparing it. Potlucks wouldn't seem right without macaroni and cheese, nor would church socials. In the Bayou, they wouldn't dream of having Thanksgiving and Christmas turkey without a big pan of macaroni and cheese alongside.

In recent years, when homey, All-American macaroni and cheddar or American cheese seemed a little unexciting and old-fashioned compared to the more exotic cheeses and pastas our specialty shops were offering, no one gave up on it. They just gave it a fancier name, made it with mozzarella, pecorino, Gruyère, or mascarpone instead of Cheddar, and used farfalle, radiatore, penne, or cavatappi instead of elbow macaroni. Whether it's called mac and cheese, *pasta con formaggio*, or *macaronis au gratin*, it is still macaroni and cheese, and it's good. No, it's great!

To love macaroni and cheese is understandable—it's very, very simple to prepare, delectable to eat, and easy to be passionate about. Wherever my travels take me, I inevitably end up with some variation of macaroni and cheese. Pasta and cheese are such perfect companions that wherever you find both cheese and pasta in a region's diet, you'll find it whipped up into its own distinctive version of macaroni and cheese.

In Britain and Ireland, for example, macaroni and cheese—known on those green isles as "macaroni cheese"—is made with the zingy Cheddars of England, Wales, Scotland, and Ireland; sometimes a little Stilton might be tossed in, too.

In Paris you might find a simple macaroni mixed with grated cheese alongside a ratatouille, or a daub of lamb. On the other hand, your *macaronis au gratin* might be brought out in a sizzling little ramekin in the trendiest restaurants—oh, la la, the cream, the cèpes, the shallots, and the Gruyerè! Or you might fork into a macaroni and cheese that is at once sleek, modern, and trendy.

From France, hop over to Switzerland, where making and eating cheese is a way of life and beautiful, well-kept cows dot the landscape, eating grass and fragrant herbs and getting ready for milking. You won't go far there without eventually dining on hearty macaroni, rich with Emmenthal or Appenzeller, studded with bits of mountain ham, and baked until the top is crusty and the inside creamy and smooth.

Or visit Germany—say, Bavaria—during the time in September when the cows come home from their summer spent in the mountains. They have eaten sweet herbs and greens and their milk is very special; villages along their path gather to welcome them, and celebrate with cheese parties and milking for a special cheese, Berkase. It is wonderful in mac and cheese: smooth and sleek, yet deliciously meltable, in the same tradition as any Gruyère, yet with its own fragrant character.

Stop in Spain for *macarrones* with manchego, chorizo, lusty peppers, and olives. And don't over-look Greece for one of the most seductive of all macaroni and cheeses: pastitsio, a layering of pasta, meat sauce, and kasseri-rich custard. Once you try it, you'll become a regular. It's inevitable.

In Turkey I ate wide, flat noodles that were stuffed with green onions, fresh dill, yogurt, and feta, topped with kashkaval, and baked to a crisp. In the Balkans I found similar dishes, but sometimes the herbs were replaced with cabbage or the pasta was dusted generously with sugar.

Dine in Italy, the spiritual home of *maccheroni con formaggio,* and you could eat your favorite dish in one guise or another nearly every day of the year. Indeed, in the mid-1800s, macaroni and cheese was the favored street food of Naples (the city that is credited with being the first to shape a paste of flour and water into fat, hollow macaroni rather than long strings and ribbons, such as spaghetti, cappellini, and fettucine). Vendors traveled the cobbled, twisting streets of old Naples, ladling up hot, steamy macaroni from a big vat, and mixing in freshly grated cheese with enough of the cooking water to make a sauce. It was called *maccheroni col due,* "for 2 cents," because that's all it cost and because you got two ingredients: macaroni and its partner in perfection, *formaggio,* or cheese.

Closer to home, when you think of *cocina mexicana,* extend your reach past the usual suspects of tacos, tortillas, and rice and beans. Spoon up a bowl of *sopa seca de fideos*—thin, short lengths of pasta, cooked in broth with chorizo, vegetables, salsa, and cheese. And then there are the surprises from here, there, and everywhere: the jolt of delight from a sweet pudding of noodles and creamy cheese, squiggles of cornstarch noodles served with ricotta cheese sorbet, or mozzarella in a cilantro-and-mint-dressed macaroni salad.

I yearn for macaroni and cheese if I'm returning home from far-flung adventures and I need soothing; I make macaroni and cheese when I have ten minutes to get something warm and inviting on the table, and when I discover a new and invigorating cheese. But most of the time, I make macaroni and cheese simply to put a smile on my eaters' faces.

Indeed, macaroni and cheese is a perfect dish to serve almost any and everybody, as long as they are not vegan, allergic to dairy products, or counting carbs or fat. It's just right for you and your spouse, parents, children, grandparents, aunt and uncle, lover, ex-lover, boss, employees, sister or brother, vicar, rabbi, guru, gardener, doctor, veterinarian, teacher, life-style coach, colleagues, co-workers, editor, and the local firemen when they knock on your door to sell tickets to their ball. And it is so affordable (well, depending on how deluxe you go) you can almost always squeeze a nice pot full of macaroni and cheese from your pantry and fridge, even when finances are tight, and feed it to your book club when everyone comes over on a Tuesday night.

Since there are hundreds of pastas and thousands of cheeses, there is a macaroni and cheese combination for every taste, from down-home to sophisticated, rich and creamy to zesty or brightly austere. Likewise, there is a macaroni and cheese dish for every purpose and occasion. To soothe the inner beast or quell the pain of a broken heart, make macaroni and cheese. Because your favorite movie is on television or twenty days on low-carb has made you crazy, only macaroni and cheese will do. You want macaroni and cheese because what could possibly be better?

The next time you find yourself alone in the kitchen wondering what's for dinner, fill a pot of water and place it on the stove over high heat. Fling open your fridge to see what kind of cheese you have, and start grating. And hopefully, by the time you have a nice pile of fragrant grated cheese ready to be melted, you'll be on your way to the best bowl of mac and cheese you've ever eaten.

Macaroni and cheese is one of life's perfect couplings: chewy, supple pasta and hearty, flavorful cheese. Each is delicious on its own, but together, as mac and cheese, they form a delicious whole so much larger than the sum of its parts. Mac and cheese is basically a simple dish: Boil the macaroni, grate the cheese, toss them together. And that's it. Well, almost. We might want a creamy sauce to bind it all, which could be béchamel or, even simpler, a bit of melted butter or crème fraîche, or we might want something zesty and wild. Tossed with the right size and shape of pasta and the right cheese, these enrichments help create a macaroni and cheese dish that is seductive and suave or lively and exciting.

THE CHEESE LOVER'S MINI-GUIDE

Since each one lends its own unique flavor and melting qualities to the bowl, here is a mini-guide to choosing your cheese, or combination of cheeses. Often it is a combination that makes the best macaroni and cheese: Mostly Cheddar with a hint of blue and Parmesan is the best combo I know for a classic rendition with some oomph. On the other hand, fewer combinations are more luscious than mozzarella, ricotta, and Parmesan, or Appenzeller and crème fraîche.

Cheddar melts brilliantly into a mac and cheese, as do the Swiss types of cheeses, Jack, Gouda, provolone, and fontina. These are the cheeses for a quintessential macaroni and cheese experience. Sometimes, though, it's nice to have little bites of a cheese that do not melt. The Hispanic cheeses—such as Panela, Cypriot anari, or halloumi—and certain Italian and Greek country cheeses all keep their shape when cut or shredded into pieces. Once grated, they are fabulous sprinkled over and tossed into macaroni.

Delicate, subtle cheeses, on the other hand, get lost in a pot of mac and cheese. Some very creamy cheeses are good, however, as a sauce: Think of creamy-fresh goat cheese mixed with extra-virgin olive oil, or mascarpone, fromage frais, ricotta, or the Greek galatyri. Add a shower of freshly grated pecorino, Parmesan, kefalotyri, or dry Jack, and your mac and cheese is delish. The flavored light, fresh cheeses in the style of Boursin, with onions, garlic, and black pepper, are yummy simply tossed into hot spaghetti or buttered macaroni and eaten from a bowl ASAP.

Most cheeses within certain categories can be used interchangeably. If your macaroni and cheese calls for a sharp Cheddar, a Grafton from Vermont or Montgomery from Britain would be equally divine, as would a nice aged Wisconsin or a Pacific West Coast cheese, such as Ig Vella's Semi Secco. Similarly, if you usually use Gruyère and you have none on hand or want a change, treat yourself to an Emmenthal, Appenzeller, Jarlsberg, fontina, or graviera. Another example: One day I wanted to make *maccheroni con Gorgonzola* but had no Gorgonzola in my fridge. I did, however, have a little chunk of Stilton. It has now become one of my desert island foods. I don't see myself ever doing without a wedge lurking in my kitchen, so good is it in macaroni, and so simple. My Midnight Macaroni (page 40) will attest to this.

The cheese types described below are categorized by flavor and texture. They are gathered from all over the world, with the exception of the Far East lands of China, Japan, and Southeast Asia, where cheese is not part of the diet. However, from Afghanistan to Argentina, indeed, throughout the world, wherever animals are kept, their fresh milk is turned into cheese and enjoyed.

FRESH CHEESES

These are lightly cultured milk products that do not go through a ripening process. They include cottage cheese; cream cheese; Italian mascarpone; soft goat cheese from California, France, and Wales; fromage blanc; German quark; Indian panir; Italian robiola; Greek galatyri; Spanish and Hispanic requeson; as well as classic Italian ricotta. Being mild, milky, and soft, they melt into a bowl of hot buttered pasta. Some make their own sauce, and some ask for a grating of something strong and sharp, such as pecorino or Parmesan, to perk it all up.

Fresh goat's and sheep's milk cheeses are very delicate. French chèvre, American (especially California) chèvre, and UK goat cheese (especially from Wales) are all wonderful crumbled into a bowl of hot pasta. Mascarpone is like pure cream; California's Contare makes an excellent domestic one.

Manouri is a fresh sheep's milk cheese from Greece, almost cream cheese–like in its mildness; if you have some on hand, by all means dice it up and toss it into your pot! Fresh mozzarella was made for melting into seductive, chewy, pizza-style strings. Toss diced mozzarella into hot, tomato-sauced pasta with a handful of fresh basil for instant *pasta alla caprese*, a dish redolent of Naples.

PRESSED CURD CHEESES

The pressed curd hard cheeses, such as halloumi and others in this category, are delicious on a bowl of hot pasta because they don't melt; they are almost like salty, briny little breadcrumbs spread throughout the macaroni. Other pressed cheeses such as Cypriot anari, fresh pecorino, and Hispanic panela are nice sizzled and served alongside a bowl of macaroni with spicy flavors, or cubed and tossed into a zesty, spicy macaroni salad.

SEMIFRESH CHEESE

Made from pressed curds, these are milky, tangy, and fresh tasting. The Italian ricotta salata is a wonderful semifresh pressed cheese, delicious grated or shaved on top of a savory pasta or macaroni, especially a tomato-sauced one. Feta is another delicious example. The best come from Greece, Israel, and Bulgaria and are made from a combination of sheep's and goat's milk, heavier on the sheep. A good feta will be sweet and creamy, salty and tangy, briny and pungent, sharp yet mild. Other Mediterranean and Balkan cheeses, such as the Turkish Beyaz Peynir, Romanian brynza, and the Spanish queso de Burgos, fall into this group too. All melt partially and are delicious in both hot and cold pasta dishes, crumbled and tossed in or layered in a baked dish.

DOUBLE- AND TRIPLE-CRÈMES

Double- and triple-crèmes have 60 percent and 75 percent butterfat, respectively. Lusciously rich, they can be either young or ripened to a nicely assertive character, such as Boursault, Saint André, Brillat-Savarin, Explorateur, and Vignottes. A few spoonfuls of a cheese like this eaten in a bowl with hot buttered pasta makes instant macaroni and cheese, and an elegant one at that. More robust-flavored, oozy cheeses, such as Saint Marcellin or Felician, do not shine in a bowl of macaroni. To enjoy these cheeses, smear them across a slab of *pain levain* or a crisp slice of baguette.

MILD AND EASILY MELTED

These all-purpose cheeses are mild in flavor and softly supple to semifirm in texture. The list includes Dutch Edam and Gouda, Hispanic mennonita and asadero, Bel Paese, Muenster, and domestic or Danish fontina (the Italian original has a much more assertive flavor and firmer consistency). And when it comes to Jack cheese, Ig Vella's Jack is always, deservedly, a prize winner. These are great cheeses for the macaroni pot! Provolone, Provatura, and scamorza are all mild Italian cheeses and are terrific in macaroni and cheese.

SOFT, FLAVORFUL CHEESES

Softish, ripened, flavorful cheeses include Reblochon, tommes, chaumes, and Tomme de Montagne. The cheeses developed over centuries in Europe's monasteries belong in this group as well: Port Salut, Saint Paulin, Esrom, Tilsit, and Havarti taste somewhat similar, while Taleggio and Stracchino can be blatantly stinky. Most in this category, which stretches to include the stronger Limburger, Stinking Bishop, Maroilles, Livarot, Pont l'Eveque, and Epoisses, will hijack your macaroni and cheese. So before you add one to your pot, ask yourself if you really want it. Taste a mouthful of pasta and a nibble of cheese. Put them in your mouth together, then make your decision.

Similarly, the bloomy rind cheeses such as Camembert, Brie, Coulommiers , Affinois, and Pavé d'Affinois, as well as the wonderful small cheeses with their fine flavors, such as Northern California's Andante Dairy, Marin French Cheese Company, or Cowgirl Creamery cheeses, get lost when their fate is thrown together with macaroni. Like many other exquisite morsels, they are meant to be savored on their own or warmed slightly and served on a crisp piece of good bread rather than in a cooked dish. No doubt there are exceptions. My personal favorite is diced ripe Camembert or Brie tossed into hot buttered pasta, then sprinkled with chopped chives.

BIG CHEESES WITH HOLES

Swiss cheeses and Swiss-style cheeses are simply a match made in heaven for macaroni. Grated and tossed with macaroni and then baked into a creamy, bubbling, sizzling, zesty casserole of pasta and melted cheese, they reach their raison d'être (well, one of them, as they're also wonderful in grilled cheese sandwiches and au gratin dishes, as well as bubbling divinely atop a bowl of savory hot onion soup).

These firmish cheeses are huge, with tough, hard rinds and interiors dotted with holes; some have many large holes and others a mere scattering of holes so tiny that they are more like Champagne bubbles. The holes are caused by the expansion of gas within the cheese curd during the ripening period. Emmenthal is probably the most famous Swiss cheese, with its distinctive holes or "eyes" and characteristically mild, nutty flavor with fruity undertones. Relatives of Emmenthal include the zesty Appenzeller and Gruyère; which are more assertive than Emmenthal, have creamier interiors, and are perfection melted into anything. Comté is the French member of the family, sweeter than Gruyère; it has been made for the past 1,000 years. Raclette has a whiff of morbier to it and is delicious melted, especially in the classic dish raclette, in which boiled potatoes are served with hot melty cheese and tiny cornichons. Vacherin Fribourgeois is softer and creamier than Gruyère, with a great depth of nutty, fruity flavor, and is lovely melted in a macaroni dish, especially with mountain ham. Beaufort is the

French "Swiss cheese" known as the prince of Gruyères; it's aged for between five and eighteen months, and its hazelnut aroma seduces while its full flavor satisfies. Norwegian Jarlsberg is a member of the family and a great workhorse for melting, though less complex and tender than the Swiss and French cheeses. Graviera, from Greece, is the exotic member of the Swiss family, with the taste and texture the Gruyère family is famous for and the whiff of far-off fields of Mediterranean herbs, which the grazing animals turn into the sweet milk that becomes this classic Greek melting cheese. When buying from this family of cheeses, do yourself a favor and don't even think of mainstream ordinary Swiss cheese. Purchase well-made, artisanal cheeses, freshly cut, that your cheesemonger lets you sample. You will be rewarded with nutty, grassy flavors that burst upon your palate.

FIRM AND FULL-FLAVORED CHEESES

Firm, full-flavored cheeses are all great in macaroni and cheese: Golden, firm, flavorful, yet not stinking, these cheeses melt deliciously. They may be made from cow's, goat's, or sheep's milk, or a combination of all three. Look for Dutch Gouda, French Tomme de Savoie, Spanish manchego, Mahón, Idiazábal, Ossau-Iraty Brebis, Italian fontina, California's Fiscalini San Joaquin Gold, medium Asiago (younger and therefore softer and more moist than aged Asiago, which is best for grating) caciocavallo, Montasio, and Ig Vella's delectable mezzo secco, a partially aged Sonoma Jack and an American gem.

THE CHEDDARS

Think of macaroni and cheese, and the image of a big hunk of Cheddar probably floats before your eyes. One of the most popular and widely made cheeses in the world, Cheddar is, in fact, a whole family of cheeses that are cheddared: In the process of cheese making, the young cheeses-in-progress are cut into pieces, stacked, and turned in the bottom of the cheese vat. Then the aging is continued. The best Cheddar will be firm in texture, with a clear, mellow taste and a nice jolt of its characteristic flavor. Cheddar is sold young (mild) and mature (sharp) as well as in several stages in between. When young, Cheddar is mild, softish, and slightly rubbery and squishy. As it matures it develops a sharp and tangy bite as well as an element of dry crumbliness.

Cheddar is a creamy pale-yellow tinged with gold in Britain, Ireland, New Zealand, and Canada, but it is often colored orange in the United States (the coloring is annatto, a spice used for tinting of many different foods). The exception is Colby Cheddar, which is marbled with both white and orange. The United States makes delicious Cheddars—Vermont, in particular, but the Pacific Northwest and Wisconsin produce some wonderful Cheddars, too.

Britain boasts a wealth of Cheddar cheeses: Montgomery's farmhouse Cheddar is divine, though many prefer Keen's; both are excellent. I'm fond of Scottish Mull of Kintyre cheese right now, as well as Dunlop, which is a Cheddar type. Gloucester, Cheshire, Leicester, Lancashire, Derby, Wensleydale, and Caerphilly all belong to the Cheddar family. Wensleydale and Caerphilly, however, are far tangier and crumblier, and less meltable. They are delicious paired with a richer, more meltable Cheddar in any pot of mac and cheese.

Cantal and mimolette are two French Cheddar types of cheeses, though very different in flavor and color (Cantal is pale yellow, mimolette bright orange). You might not recognize Cantal's connection with the Cheddar family, but the mimolette is obvious. The Greek kashkaval is a cheese made with a cheddaring technique, but since it is made from sheep's milk, the flavor is far more like a pecorino than a Cheddar. Kashkaval is a cheese to keep in mind when you're thinking macaroni and cheese.

HARD, SHARP CHEESES

Cheeses for grating are all known for their exceptionally hard texture and strong, sharp taste. These include Parmesan; aged Asiago; Romano; pecorino; mountain cheeses from the Greek islands, such as myzithra and kefalotyri; Grana Padano; dry Jack, Sprinz; Cotija; and enchilado. Some, such as Parmesan, have a slightly nutty flavor.

BLUE-VEINED CHEESES

Blue-veined cheeses are great tossed into a pot of pasta, either on their own or with other ingredients or cheeses. Pungent and tangy, this family is characterized by its blue-green or green veins, formed after the cheese is inoculated with a penicillium spore. They can vary from soft to quite crumbly in texture. Roquefort, Fourme d'Ambert, Bleu des Causses, Stilton, Gorgonzola, Cabrales, Blue Castello, Spanish Picón, American Point Reyes, Maytag Blue, Rogue River blues, Danish and Swedish blues, and some of the German sharp village blues are all great, assertive cheeses. Scotland produces some wonderful blues (if you can get your hands on a true Lanarkshire blue, treat yourself to a heavenly nibble), as does Ireland (Cashel) and England (besides the rich Stilton, Oxford blue is pungent and divine). And if you have a chance to sample it, Shropshire is a delicious blue-veined English Cheddar.

GOAT AND SHEEP CHEESES

Distinctively different in taste from cow's milk cheeses—the phrase "whiff of the barnyard" comes to mind—goat and sheep cheese may be fresh and tangy, or formed and aged in a variety of sizes and shapes. Both are formed into pyramids, cones, and discs, while goat cheese is often sold in cylinders, as well. The shapes are not merely for esthetics. They offer a variety of surface exposures and thus affect aging and ripening. The same milk mixture formed into different shapes will age differently and thus taste differently. Often cheeses are known by their specific shape, such as the Valençay, with its distinctive pyramid with the top chopped off. Occasionally, goat and sheep cheeses are wrapped in vine or other fragrant leaves, such as the chestnut-leaf-wrapped goat's or cow's milk Banon. They are also covered in ash or mold, such as the tiny crottins made of goat's milk with herbs, or the rosemary-coated sheep's milk brin d'amour from the south of France.

Pecorino is another sheep cheese (*pecora* means "sheep" in Italian). It is one of Italy's most delectable, especially the pecorino of Tuscany, where it is eaten in many different stages, from young and tender and full of pungency and tang, to hard and ready to be grated into a bowl of pasta. Sheep cheeses are sometimes large, especially if they are to be aged or mixed with either cow's or goat's milk and then aged. Idiazábal and Ossau-Iraty Brebis from the Basque Country are all sheep's milk, while Spain's manchego can be a mixture of sheep's, goat's, and cow's milk.

SPICED OR FLAVORED CHEESES

Flavored cheeses can be mighty tasty in mac and cheese. Hot pepper Jack, garlic Jack, nettle Gouda, cumin-scented Leyden, onion and chive Double Gloucester, dill-speckled Havarti, and Sage Derby with its herbal aroma can each add its savor to the right macaroni and cheese. As for truffled pecorino, just grate that into any pot of pasta, add a hit or two of truffle oil if you like, pick up your spoon, and prepare to swoon.

SMOKED CHEESES

Many different cheeses, such as scamorza, provolone, Cheddar, Gouda, and mozzarella, are treated with wood smoke, either naturally, by hanging them over a fireplace, or unnaturally, by coating the outside of the cheese with liquid smoke. I find the latter far too harsh. Even when the smoky flavor is rather piquant, I would avoid these in a macaroni and cheese—with the exception of smoked provolone or mozzarella, which are delicious diced into a lusty tomato-and-meat-sauced macaroni.

PROCESSED CHEESES

Processed cheese is usually made from several different cheese types blended together. Cutting into the aging cheese disturbs its microbacterial growth, and the heat and disruption of the blending stops it dead in its tracks. Because of this, it can never develop character as does a naturally produced cheese. Many classic recipes for macaroni and cheese call for this processed, or American, type of cheese because it melts easily into an oozy, gooey sauce. But why use a manufactured cheese product when the world is full of wonderful real cheeses, made by real people, using good milk and traditional, time-honored, natural methods? And they taste so delicious when melted into your pot of pasta.

BUYING AND STORING

Go directly to the best cheese shop you can find and make friends with the owners. Return regularly to taste, taste, and taste some more. Try a recipe with one cheese, and the next time you make the dish, try another cheese. Most shops will encourage your sampling and discoveries. This is how to get the best cheese education you'll ever find. In the process, you'll learn that cheese is seasonal, and the way it is kept and treated will, much like wine, influence its flavor, aroma, and texture. The mutual interest between cheese maker/seller and cheese eater will enhance your education and enjoyment.

In Europe, many cheese shops are also *affineurs*, specialists in aging cheeses as well as vendors who sell them. Increasingly, cheese shops and some restaurants in the United States are aging cheeses, too. Properly aged, cheeses grow from being good to memorable.

Some well-stocked supermarkets carry an excellent selection of cheeses. Though many are wonderful, some will be phantoms of their more flavorful selves because of overly cold storage en route to the shops. Even when the temperature has been carefully calibrated, sitting cut-up and plastic-wrapped on the shelves has sent these cheeses into a state of hibernation, and they will never be as delicious as cheese that is cut for you directly from a big wheel or round.

These days, farmers' markets often sell artisanal cheeses. Some of the cheese makers at these markets have farms you can visit to see the animals and taste the cheeses. It's a wonderful way to learn to understand and love the whole close-to-nature character of cheese.

Once purchased, cheese should be stored in a cool place. Even though different cheeses prefer different temperatures, the refrigerator is a good place to store them all.

Cheese should also be protected from moisture loss. Wrapping it with plastic film is good for the short term. Plastic does not let the cheese breathe, however, and bacteria builds up on the cheese's surface, threatening spoilage. If you are using plastic wrap on a whole, large cheese, cover only the cut area. This protects the cut surface but lets the natural rind on the outside breathe the way a cheese is meant to.

Wrap blue cheeses in foil first and then cover loosely with plastic. When tightly wrapped in plastic, they sweat unpleasantly. Change the plastic every few days to keep the cheese dry.

Specially designed glass bells resting on a plate or plastic containers are good, but take care when storing different cheeses together. Never store blue cheese or any other strong cheese with milder ones, because the strong blue bacteria spores migrate and turn anything near it bluish. In addition, all cheeses should be individually wrapped in plastic to prevent errant bacteria from one cheese from imparting their distinctive—and probably unwanted—flavor to the cheese next to it.

NEXT CHOOSE YOUR MACARONI

Different cheeses demand different pasta. Which one to choose from the literally hundreds of shapes? In general, there are two basic types: chunky macaroni, and long strings and ribbons of spaghetti and tagliatelle.

Thin strands of pasta are delicious—who doesn't love spaghetti?—but strings of pasta are at their best slicked down with olive oil, snuggled with seafood or sausage, bitten with spice, or blanketed with a sauce of olive oil or tomatoes, then tossed with gratings of salty dry cheese, such as Parmesan. For most macaroni and cheese, you usually want a chunky macaroni that can take the heft of creamy sauce and rich cheese. Long lengths of pasta can get weighed down, or worse yet, the cheese may clump together. There are delicious exceptions, though, such as Penne con Cacio e Pepe (page 35), which can be made with either penne or spaghetti tossed with a sauce of extra-virgin olive oil, black pepper, and tons of freshly grated pecorino or Parmesan.

Italians usually refer to short, thick pasta as *maccheroni*, which was first made in what is now the Naples area. It was originally formed—records show around 1279—by rolling dough around knitting needles. This fat pasta holds on to the cheese best, and is able to withstand baking with a rich sauce and melting cheese. Some *maccheroni*, such as penne, ziti, and ditali, are smooth, while others are ridged. The tiny lines are meant to help sauce cling to the pasta and give the dish more texture. Flat egg noodles make great macaroni and cheese, too; whether wide or narrow, they cradle the melting cheese deliciously. Think of the classic tuna-noodle casserole.

Here, then, is a little guide to the macaroni that will take pride of place in your mac and cheese. Since there are hundreds of different shapes of this delectable food, each crafted in a different style and wearing a different name, you probably have your own favorite sitting in your cupboard, ready to add to this list!

Anellini: Small rings of pasta, traditionally mixed with tomato sauce, sausage, and cheese, then baked until bubbly. Anellini may also be stirred into a light soup.

Alphabetti: Tiny alphabet pastina, eaten in soup.

Bucatini: Long strands of pasta, spaghetti-like in their length, but fat and hollow. It is good in any casserole of tomato and cheese and is also a favorite for Greek Pastitsio (page 111).

Cavateppi: Corkscrew spirals, terrific with melty cheese in a mac and cheese.

Cicatelli: These are half hollow, half open, somewhat chewy, and about three inches long.

Conchiglie: Literally, "shells." Shell-shaped pasta come in a wide variety of sizes, from the huge beasts (conchiglioni), which are delicious stuffed, to little finger-sized shells, which are perfect for soup. The smaller to medium shells are best in most macaroni and cheeses, and are especially good in macaroni salad. Gnocchetti and cavatelli are similar cup- or shell-shaped pastas that can be substituted for conchiglie.

Couscous: A North African pasta. These tiny grains are traditionally eaten with meats and spicy sauce.

Ditalini: Literally, "little fingertips." Ditalini are short, squat macaroni the size of, well, the tip of your finger. They're good in soup and great tossed with cheese—pretty much all purpose lovely little pasta. Ditali are somewhat bigger.

Elbow macaroni: Somewhat curved, this short, hollow, tubular macaroni comes in a variety of sizes, from an inch or so, with a substantial hole in the center, to a tiny little pasta, called maccheroncini, with a pin-sized hole going through. Regardless of its size, elbow is a macaroni of choice for many a mac and cheese, from big cheesy panfuls to mayo-and-relish-spiked mac and Cheddar salad. Elbow macaroni are mac and cheese workhorses; there are few mac and cheeses that these little macaroni are not perfect for.

Farfalle: "Butterfly" in Italian. The name refers to the butterfly or bow-tie-shaped flat pastas that are so delicious in almost any type of macaroni and cheese. Although they are usually medium-large, you can sometimes find tiny butterfly shapes that are nice in soups and in creamy, almost risotto-like mac and cheeses.

Fettucine: These flat ribbons of pasta are delicious with many cheese sauces.

Fusilli: Pasta twists, which are delicious vehicles for macaroni and cheese. Spinach or tricolor vegetable fusilli are particularly nice in a variety of mac and cheese ways.

Gemelli: Literally, "twins." They consist of two intertwined thickish strands, about three inches long.

Gigli: Literally, "lilies." These are lily-shaped pasta with noodle dough fanning out from a pinched end. They are good anywhere that shells or noodles are suggested.

Lasagne: Wide, flat noodles. Lasagne are brilliant for layering with sauces and cheeses. A casserole of lasagne, béchamel, and layers of gooey cheese is probably the ultimate mac and cheese, if you love all things Italian.

Lumache: Literally, "snails." These are, of course, snail-shaped pasta; lumachine are a smaller version.

Malloreddus: A partially closed, chewy, dumpling-like pasta from Sardinia, similar to cicatelli.

Noodles: Wide egg noodles are delicate and on the thin side and are delicious for layering with cottage cheese, feta, and yogurt mixtures in Turkish or Balkan dishes. Thinner noodles are choice for a good *lokshen kugel* (page 125), the Jewish Eastern European specialty made with noodles, cottage cheese, and sweet flavors.

Occhi di lupo or *occhi di trota:* Literally, "eyes of the world" or "eyes of the trout." These are two variations of ditali. The first is larger than ditali, and the second is smaller.

Orecchiette: Thick pasta whose Italian name translates as "little ears," a reference to the tender cup shape of the dough. Orecchiette are good with vegetables such as broccoli and are very nice served as a macaroni salad with lemon juice and arugula.

Orzo: Rice-shaped pasta. Delish in soup, or just buttered and blanketed with grated Parmesan.

Pappardelle: Wide Italian noodles, good sauced and layered with a robust sauce and cheese.

Pastina: These tiny pasta, almost grainlike in their diminutive size, are at their best eaten in soup. Sometimes pastina are wonderful with a bit of grated cheese, but they are too delicate to withstand the onslaught of a heavy sauce. Pastina includes alphabetti ("alphabets"), semi di melone ("melon seeds"), ancini di pepe ("peppercorns"), and stelline ("little stars").

Penne: Penne are quill-shaped pasta, chewy, sturdy, and delightfully hollow for capturing a nice mouthful of cheese when you toss it into the bowl. Penne come in a wide variety of sizes, from pennette, the tiny ones, to penne regine, the large, queen-sized version.

Pizzocheri: Ribbons of hefty, hearty buckwheat pasta, pizzocheri is eaten in Italy's Alpine region, Valtellina, traditionally layered with cabbage and cheese.

Radiatore: Literally, "radiators." These pasta do bear an uncanny resemblance to radiators, with ruffles of pasta around their middles that deliciously trap sauce. Radiatore are good in anything that calls for rotelle (see below).

Rigatoni: Smooth or ridged, these fat and relatively short tubes tend to flap about in their sauce.

Rotelle: Wheel-shaped pasta. Rotelle are good with chunky, thick sauces as this is a sturdy little pasta. Serve rotelle with rich, tomatoey sauce and a layer of cheese, almost like lasagne. Toss them with béchamel and as much cheese as you dare—the little rotelle are up for the job!

Strozzapreti: The name means "priest-strangler." As legend has it, the local priest ate so many, because of course it was so delicious, that he choked! Strozzapreti are made without eggs, just flour and water, and may look like fat spaghetti, or even fatter, more rustic squiggles.

Trofie: Trofie are knots, thin at one end and fat at the other, giving a nice variety of textures in one bite of chewy pasta. A Ligurian specialty, they are traditionally eaten with pesto, and are good with a ground nut and mascarpone sauce as well.

Ziti: Tubular pasta, longer and thinner than rigatoni.

HOW TO COOK PASTA: SECRETS OF SUCCESS

1 Allow lots and lots of rapidly boiling water, say 1½ quarts for 1 pound of dried pasta. The hot bubbling water needs to cover the pasta, getting into every nook and cranny, cooking it evenly, and draining all the excess starch away. Without enough boiling water, the pasta will be gummy and bloated, with some errant bits here and there still hard and crunchy.

2 Be sure the water is really rolling at a boil before you put the pasta in. This cooks the outside of the pasta immediately and gives a nice smooth edge to it. If the water is not hot enough, your pasta will be mushy.

3 When you add the pasta, the water will stop boiling for a moment or two. Stir the pasta gently so that it doesn't stick together in one blob while waiting for the water to come to the boil again. When it returns to the boil, lower the heat slightly so that the water and pasta cook together at a moderate boil—if they cook *too* furiously, the water may boil over.

4 Be sure there is enough salt in the water, about 1 tablespoon per quart of water. Some say the salt is added to maintain the water at the boiling point, but others maintain the salt has no effect and its function is pure flavor. Regardless, you're pouring it off when you drain the pasta, and without enough salt in the cooking water, the pasta tastes bland.

5 Don't add oil to the water; it weighs the pasta down. If you want your pasta lightly touched with olive oil, toss it with a little oil *after* you drain it.

6 Never overcook! Pasta generally needs to cook slightly less than the time called for on the package. I always start testing at about halfway through the cooking time. Pasta is ready when it shows a little bit of resistance to the teeth as you chomp into it. This is called *al dente*, which literally means "to the teeth." If you're eating the pasta right away, drain it and serve. If you're returning it to the stove top and the pasta is going to cook a little bit longer, drain it when the pasta is *almost* al dente and then return it to the pot. And, finally, if you're going to toss the pasta with sauce, then cheese, then bake it to a bubbly, savory casserole, drain the pasta when it still has a tiny bit of crunch as you bite down into a piece of the partially cooked pasta. About two-thirds of the cooking time recommended on the package should be fine. If the pasta cooks particularly quickly, half the suggested time will be good.

PUTTING IT TOGETHER

When I'm in the mood for macaroni and cheese without any preplanning, I just peruse my cupboard to see which shapes I've got on hand, put up the water to boil, and start grating. Sometimes my best bowls of mac and cheese come about in that serendipitous way!

In other words:

1 Boil and drain the pasta.
2 Shred the cheese.
3 Toss the two together quickly, and eat hot!

That is the simplest of creations, the one you're most apt to curl up with on a Saturday night along with a good movie and the cat, or put on the table after a long, hard day at work.

For a classic macaroni and cheese, in which the macaroni is encased in a creamy, cheesy sauce, you'll need to make a béchamel sauce (page 28). Béchamel, or its Italian sibling *besciamella*, is simply another, though definitely classier, way of saying "white sauce."

Béchamel Sauce

Makes enough for 12 to 16 ounces of macaroni, depending on what else you're adding.

Béchamel can be doubled, tripled, or quadrupled, or reduced in the same way. As long as the proportions are the same, the sauce will be fine. An excellent shortcut for heating the milk is to use the microwave: Place it in the microwave right in its glass measuring cup and zap it for 1½ minutes on High. Heating the milk before adding it to the cooked flour makes it easier to dissolve the floury lumps in the sauce. Or you can simply add the milk cold. To be honest, this is what I do. You'll need a whisk at hand, however, to whisk away those inevitable lumps. For a thicker béchamel, increase the amount of fat and flour by half or double it; for a thinner béchamel, decrease the amount of fat and flour by about half.

Béchamel thickens even more as it cools, and loosens again as it heats (but never gets as thin as it is when you first make it). For a velouté, which is a more savory sauce (good for tuna or seafood casserole), make a béchamel with half milk and half broth—chicken, seafood, or vegetable.

1½ tablespoons butter or extra-virgin olive oil

1½ to 2 tablespoons flour

1½ cups hot, but not boiling, milk (whole milk is traditional, but low-fat milk—not nonfat—is just fine)

Salt to taste

A pinch of cayenne pepper or white pepper (black is fine if you don't mind the dark flecks)

A grating of fresh nutmeg

In a heavy-bottomed nonstick saucepan, melt the butter or warm the olive oil. Don't let the butter brown.

Sprinkle in the flour evenly, then cook for 30 seconds to 1 minute over medium-low heat; this cooks away the raw quality of the flour. (If you don't cook the flour your sauce will be gluey; cooking the flour will give you a smooth, thick sauce.) Stir together and continue to cook for half a minute or so; you don't want to brown the flour, but a pale gold color will give you a more toasty flavor.

Remove the pan from the heat and add the hot milk all at once. Stir to combine and begin to dissolve the flour and fat, then return to the heat and cook, stirring with a wooden spoon all the while, as the sauce becomes smooth and begins to thicken. Season with the salt, pepper, and nutmeg once the sauce has thickened. When it is thick, it is ready.

REASONS TO EAT MACARONI AND CHEESE

You're hungry.

You're happy.

You want to be happy.

You got a raise! Celebrate.

You got fired! Mac and cheese is excellent for comfort.

New job! Hard work, little time. Mac and cheese for supper, definitely!

You broke up with your boyfriend/girlfriend and need to drown your sorrows in pasta and cheese.

You've met Mr./Ms. Right and want to feed him/her your favorite food.

The weather is cold and foggy.

You're feeling lonely. Mac and cheese makes everything feel okay again.

You're feeling overwhelmed with people and want to be alone with your dinner.

Your Netflix has arrived—you're ready for dinner and a movie or three.

You're having brined pork chops for dinner, and nothing is as good with pork chops as macaroni and cheese.

You're not having pork chops because you are a vegetarian or you keep halal/kosher, and macaroni and cheese is such a wonderful vegetarian dish.

Tomorrow you're going low-carb, low-fat.

'Cause you love it!

The mac and cheeses in this chapter are easy, as in start a pot of water heating on the stove, look over the pastas in your cupboard, and fling open your fridge to check out your cheeses. Though the recipes are designed to serve four, these are easygoing, freewheeling cheesy potfuls you can whip up at any time of the day or night. You might only be two, rather than four, to share the pot, or it might be you dining on macaroni and cheese solo. Therefore, all recipes can be halved to serve two, or quartered to serve one, happily, easily, and deliciously.

Five Easy Mac and Cheeses

Ravioli al Forno: Cook 1 pound of ravioli (choose any filling—I like spinach in this dish) until al dente. Drain and layer in a baking dish with 2 cups of diced tomatoes (canned is fine); 3 cloves of garlic, chopped; 1 or 2 teaspoons of chopped fresh rosemary; and about 12 ounces of sliced provolone, Jack, kasseri, or any pale-colored easily melted cheese. Drizzle with olive oil, sprinkle with Parmesan, and bake in a 375°F oven until the cheeses melt and the whole thing sizzles and browns lightly.

Chorizo and Goat Cheese: Toss al dente macaroni with a little olive oil and garlic, then with matchstick slices of salami-like cured Spanish chorizo and dollops of tangy fresh goat cheese. Serve right away.

Tiny Elbows with Ripe Camembert or Brie, Scented with Chives: Cook 3½ to 4 ounces of small elbow macaroni until al dente. Drain and toss the hot macaroni with 2½ to 3 ounces of ripe Camembert or Brie, cut into small pieces. The cheese will partially melt from the heat of the pasta. When softened, sprinkle with a teaspoon or two of chopped chives and sea salt to taste. Eat in a warm bowl.

Truffles, Peas, Pasta, and Cheese: Treat yourself to a jar of truffle *condimiento* (with or without porcini). It won't be cheap, but it will give you gorgeous truffle flavor—and hey, you are worth it! Toss spoonfuls of the fragrant paste into hot, buttered, al dente pasta, to which you added a handful of peas at the last minute of cooking. Shower with shredded mild pecorino or Asiago.

Sun-Dried Tomato and Goat Cheese Penne: Finely chop a couple of oil-packed sun-dried tomatoes and mix in a bowl with an ounce or two of fresh tangy goat cheese, a pinch of thyme, a clove or two of crushed or chopped garlic, and about 3 tablespoons of extra-virgin olive oil, and mix until it forms a chunky, creamy paste. Cook about 6 ounces of penne until al dente, drain, and toss with the sun-dried tomato and goat cheese mixture. Eat right away.

ALPINE MACARONI AND APPENZELLER WITH CRÈME FRAÎCHE

Nutty and slightly spicy, Appenzeller is one of the classic cheeses for a luscious Swiss fondue, along with Emmenthal and Gruyère; they are all good cheeses to use in this dish. From across the French border, Comté is also a delicious choice.

Accompany the dish with a light and leafy green salad: young mâche, baby lettuces, chopped chives, and chervil if you've any around; otherwise, toss in a little chopped parsley. For dessert, I'd slice oranges and serve them dusted with sugar and cinnamon if it is winter or, for summer, melon chunks—pink watermelon, pale green honeydew, and sunset-hued cantaloupe—sprinkled with lime juice and zest and some fresh mint.

Cook the pasta in a large pot of rapidly boiling salted water until it is al dente. Drain, and reserve about 1 cup of the cooking liquid.

Return the hot pasta to the pan immediately, and toss with the garlic, shallot, shredded cheese sprinkled evenly over the top, crème fraîche, nutmeg, salt and pepper, and butter. Ladle in about ¼ cup of the cooking liquid and toss gently. If the cheese doesn't melt right away, turn the heat to low for a few moments; the cooking liquid should help produce a light, saucy coating of cheese for the pasta. If it seems dry, ladle in a bit more of the liquid.

12 ounces smallish macaroni, such as elbows or pennette

2 cloves garlic, chopped

1 shallot, chopped

10 to 12 ounces Appenzeller, Emmenthal, Gruyère, or Comté cheese, shredded

4 ounces crème fraîche, or as desired

A grating of fresh nutmeg

Salt and freshly ground black pepper to taste

2 to 3 tablespoons unsalted butter

MACARONI AND CHEESE
FOR PEOPLE WHO LOVE ONIONS

Serves
4

This is a quintessential macaroni and cheese, but quick as can be, and with a light touch—no béchamel sauce to hold it all together, just pure melting cheese and toothsome macaroni. If you are someone who does not love onions, simply omit and retitle the recipe, the Simplest Mac and Cheese Ever. But if you do love onions, they, along with chives, taste just perfect with all the rich, melty cheese.

I'd also serve a nice bowl of baby greens, such as mizuna, amaranth, chard, romaine, arugula, and mâche, with a scattering of walnuts and diced roasted beets or a handful of crisp purple grapes, a glistening of extra-virgin, and a drop or two of wine vinegar.

12 ounces tiny elbow macaroni (maccheroncini)

2 to 3 tablespoons heavy cream or whole milk

4 ounces sharp Cheddar cheese, shredded

4 ounces Red Leicester, Cheshire, or mimolette cheese, shredded

2 ounces sharp, pungent grating cheese, such as Parmesan, pecorino, or dry Jack, grated

Salt and freshly ground black or cayenne pepper to taste

1 small to medium red onion, or 2 shallots, finely chopped

1 bunch chives, chopped

Cook the pasta in a large pot of rapidly boiling salted water until just tender. Drain, and reserve a few spoonfuls of the cooking liquid.

Return the hot drained pasta to the hot pan. Sprinkle with the cream, then start sprinkling with the cheeses, adding a little bit at a time, and then tossing with the macaroni. If you add too much cheese at one time, the shreds will migrate toward each other and melt together into one big cheese lump. You want the cheese tossed throughout the pasta. Add a tablespoon or two of the cooking water as you toss the cheese, and a spoonful or two of extra cream if needed. Season with salt and pepper, then toss in the chopped onion and the chives.

You can serve immediately, or pour into a buttered baking pan, sprinkle a little more cheese on top, and bake for 15 minutes or so in a 375°F oven until hot and sizzly.

PENNE CON CACIO E PEPE

Pasta with Lots of Cheese and Black Pepper

Serves
4

Use great quality pasta, fabulous olive oil, freshly ground black pepper, and strong, really wonderful cheese for this one. Since it's so simple, this dish is all about the ingredients, and the way the cheese and oil are combined before being tossed with the pasta. You could, of course, toss the pasta with the oil and then with the cheese, but the result won't be as brilliant. Science or magic, who knows? Perhaps a little bit of both.

This quintessential Italian macaroni and cheese is eaten all over Italy in one guise or another. In some villages, pecorino is preferred, while in others, Asiago or Parmigiano is the local choice. In some places home cooks use butter instead of oil, and sometimes they add a big pinch of hot pepper and maybe a little browned sausage. But I think, as with all classics, purity is perfection. In this recipe I call for penne, but the dish is equally traditional and delicious with spaghetti, instead.

Serve a ripe tomato salad alongside, definitely, in summer; in winter, a salad of crisp radicchio dressed in extra-virgin and lemon will be perfect. If you're forking this up in spring, serve it with a plate of lightly cooked fresh spinach, squeezed of its extra cooking liquid, and drizzled with olive oil and a few drops of wine vinegar.

Cook the pasta in a large pot of rapidly boiling salted water until al dente. Drain and reserve about 1 cup of the cooking water.

While the pasta is cooking, mix the oil with the cheese and pepper in a small to medium-size bowl; stir together well to make a cheesy mélange; ladle in ½ cup or so of the hot cooking water and mix well.

Return the drained pasta to the pot and add the cheese and oil mixture in several batches, tossing as you go. (Adding too much cheese at once will encourage it to clump together—not nice!) Add a little more of the cooking liquid if the pasta seems dry. Serve right away in shallow soup bowls, warmed if possible. Pass the extra cheese, black pepper, and salt for those who want an added kick.

1 pound penne

1 cup extra-virgin olive oil, or more as needed

4½ to 5 ounces Pecorino Romano or Parmesan cheese, grated, plus a hunk for serving

1 to 1½ teaspoons freshly ground black pepper, plus extra for serving

Salt to taste, if necessary

NIGEL'S GREEN MACARONI
WITH **BASIL** AND **GOAT CHEDDAR**

Serves
4

Nigel Patrick, my husband's oldest friend, created this recipe inspired by a goat cheese pasta dish I had once fed him. When he served it back to me with goat Cheddar—instead of the creamy, crumbly fresh goat cheese in my original—I was enchanted. Goat Cheddar is delish grated and tossed with pasta; it adds a slightly piquant edge to a familiar dish. If you've no goat Cheddar, a nice Spanish manchego is good instead.

For dessert, I might serve lemon sorbet doused with lemoncello and grappa as a cocktail-like treat. Nigel, on the other hand, would never feed a friend without organizing an evening of games afterward. I suggest both.

6 to 8 cloves garlic, chopped

6 to 8 tablespoons thinly sliced or shredded fresh basil

6 tablespoons extra-virgin olive oil

12 ounces green (spinach) shells, green and yellow tagliatelle, or fettuccine

6 tablespoons freshly grated dry Jack, pecorino, or aged Asiago cheese

8 ounces dry, aged goat Cheddar; manchego; aged Gouda; sheep's milk kasseri; or a similar cheese, cut into thin shards or shavings

Combine the garlic, basil, and olive oil in a large bowl.

Cook the pasta in a large pot of rapidly boiling salted water until al dente. Drain, reserving about 1 cup of the hot cooking liquid in case you need it for the pasta.

Toss the hot pasta with the garlic, basil, and oil in the bowl, then toss with the freshly grated dry Jack. If the pasta seems a little dry, toss with a few spoonfuls of the cooking liquid. Toss it with the shards or shavings of goat Cheddar and serve immediately.

MIDSUMMER'S MACARONI

Penne with Goat Cheese, Olives, and Thyme

It doesn't get any simpler than this: hot pasta, briny black olives or olivada (black olive paste), fresh tangy goat cheese, a fragrant pinch of thyme, and, of course, abundant garlic. As the legendary chef Louis Diat (creator of vichyssoise) once said, "Without garlic, I have no will to live." My friends and family all swear that I am the author of that quote.

I might like to serve this after a few salady meze: boiled or steamed zucchini, sliced and dressed with olive oil, lemon juice, garlic, and thyme; roasted red peppers and olives; and sliced oranges, fennel, and radishes.

If using whole olives, whirl in the food processor until they are finely chopped and put in a bowl large enough for the pasta. Or put the olivada in the bowl. Mix in the garlic, olive oil, goat cheese, and thyme.

Cook the pasta in a large pot of rapidly boiling salted water until al dente. Drain and reserve a few spoonfuls of the pasta cooking water.

Toss the hot pasta into the oil, olive, and cheese mixture. Season with the salt and pepper, and add a tablespoon or two of the hot cooking water, tossing it with the pasta to bind it with the sauce.

Eat right away!

1 **cup pitted black Mediterranean olives, or ⅔ cup olivada (black olive paste)**

3 to 4 **cloves garlic, chopped**

3 **tablespoons extra-virgin olive oil, or as desired**

6 **ounces mild goat cheese, such as chevreaux, Montrachet, or California chevre, crumbled**

½ **teaspoon fresh thyme leaves or a pinch of dried thyme, crushed between your hands to bring out the aroma and flavor**

12 **ounces penne**

Salt and freshly ground black pepper or red pepper flakes to taste

MIDNIGHT MACARONI

Garlicky Buttered Tricolor Fusilli with Stilton

Serves
4

Make a whole batch for supper, or quarter the recipe for one simple, indulgent midnight snack. Other pastas are good instead of the orange, green, and ivory twists. Try farfalle, gigli, or any green macaroni. The dish is predictably good, too, with Gorgonzola, Cabrales, Picón, Fourme d'Ambert, Bleu d'Auvergne, or a rich German blue instead of Stilton. I would avoid anything too sharp, though, as mild richness is just what you want in this bowl.

If you feel like a salad alongside, try my latest fave: finely diced celery and chopped parsley, shallots, and garlic, with a splash of extra-virgin and lemon juice and a sprinkle of salt. Refreshing and tangy, celery is a classic partner to Stilton.

12 ounces tricolor fusilli

2 to 3 cloves garlic, chopped

3 tablespoons unsalted butter, cut into ½-inch pieces

3 ounces Stilton cheese, grated, chopped, or broken up into small pieces

Salt and freshly ground black pepper to taste

Cook the pasta in a large pot of rapidly boiling salted water until al dente. Drain and reserve a few spoonfuls of the cooking water.

While the pasta is cooking, combine the garlic with the butter; no need to really mix, just put both in a large mixing bowl and give a toss or two to combine.

As soon as the pasta is drained, tip it into the butter and garlic, then add the Stilton and toss together, letting the butter and Stilton melt and mix together. Season with salt and pepper and eat right away.

MACARONI'S GOT THE BLUES

Serves
4

Well, macaroni might have the blues, but it's got pesto and cream, too, all tossed into a rich basil-scented, cream-enriched blue cheese sauce, which turns it a beautiful shade of pale green. Confusing? Not when you taste it. It's divine.

If you don't feel like toasting the pine nuts, don't bother. The dish will lack the crunch of the toasted pine nuts, but in fact will be more traditional—Ligurians never brown their pine nuts for pesto. Whether raw or toasted, the tiny, tender nut is very nice scattered on top of pasta tossed with this creamy pesto and blue cheese sauce.

¼ cup pine nuts

8 ounces fine, briny, pungent blue cheese, such as Point Reyes Blue, Maytag Blue, or Roquefort, crumbled

⅓ cup heavy cream or mascarpone

3 tablespoons good-quality pesto, home-made or store-bought

12 ounces tubular pasta, such as penne; or flat noodles or ribbons, such as tagliatelle; or trofie, that distinctive Ligurian knot

Lightly toast the pine nuts in a heavy nonstick frying pan over medium heat until the pine nuts turn golden brown in spots. Remove from heat and pour into a bowl or plate.

Meanwhile, in a large bowl, combine the blue cheese with the cream and pesto. Set aside.

Cook the pasta in a large pot of rapidly boiling salted water until al dente. Drain and reserve about ¼ cup of the cooking water.

Toss the hot pasta with the blue cheese, cream, and pesto in a large bowl, adding a few spoonfuls of the hot cooking water to bind the sauce to the pasta.

Sprinkle with the toasted pine nuts and serve right away on warmed plates.

Macaroni Is Very Green with Asparagus: Add ½ bunch (about ½ pound) of asparagus, trimmed of their tough ends and cut into 2- or 3-inch lengths, to the cooking pasta during the last minute or two. Drain and sauce along with the pasta.

THE CONTESSA'S RIGATONI

Serves
4

With its creamy porcini and sausage sauce and whiff of truffle, this pasta is as lavish and luxurious as my friend the contessa (or should I say the shy contessa—she prefers not to use her title, though I find it irresistibly exotic), who served me the dish. In any event, do as she does—serve this dish when you want to make people crazy with happiness.

Note that all truffle oils are not equal in quality. The best ones have a slice or two of truffle steeping in the bottle to keep their aroma and flavor. These are, predictably and sadly, the most expensive.

¾ cup dry white wine, such as an unoaked Chardonnay or a Pinot Grigio

1½ cups chicken or beef broth, homemade or canned

½ to ¾ ounce dried porcini mushrooms, broken up into smallish pieces

1½ to 2 sweet Italian sausages, removed from their casing and broken up into small morsels about the size of tiny meatballs

Pinch of fennel seeds (if sausages are already scented with fennel, omit the seeds)

1 cup heavy cream

12 ounces tubular pasta, such as rigatoni, penne, or ziti; or twists, such as a delicate fusilli

6 ounces pecorino cheese, grated, plus extra grated pecorino or Parmesan for serving

6 to 8 ounces fontina, Gruyère, or Appenzeller cheese, shredded

2 tablespoons truffle oil, or to taste (optional)

Salt and freshly ground black pepper to taste

In a large deep frying pan, combine the wine and broth with the porcini, broken-up sausage, and fennel seeds. Bring to a boil, over medium-high heat, then reduce the heat slightly to medium and cook at a gentle boil until the liquid has reduced by at least half, and preferably about two-thirds. The porcini will be rehydrated and the sausage pieces will be cooked through. Pour in the cream, stir well, and warm until it bubbles around the edge. Remove the sauce from the heat and cover to keep warm.

Cook the pasta in a large pot of rapidly boiling salted water until al dente. Drain, reserving about 1 cup of the cooking liquid.

Add the hot drained pasta to the large frying pan with the warm sauce and toss well, then return to the stove and warm over a low heat. Sprinkle the cheeses over the pasta in a few batches to prevent clumping, tossing each time to incorporate the cheese into the pasta and drizzling with a bit of the reserved cooking water as you toss.

Remove from heat, sprinkle with the truffle oil (if using) and season with salt and pepper. Serve right away, and offer pecorino or Parmesan to anyone who wishes.

LOKSHEN WITH CHEESE

Pasta with Cottage Cheese and Green Onions or Garlic

This eastern European Jewish dish of noodles and cottage cheese is classic any-time-of-the-day food: great for a quick supper or lunch, delish for a midnight snack, and acceptable for breakfast, too.

You can add a little chopped green onion or a whiff of garlic, as I do. But you might take after my daughter and stepdaughter and add peas to the pot. Your choice of pasta itself depends on personal preference: Chewy farfalle cradles spoonfuls of soft cheese in each bite, while the twisting shape of fusilli traps morsels of cheese in its coils. Buckwheat soba is hearty and rustic, while spaghetti is my middle-of-the-night choice. If I'm boiling tiny pasta for soup, I'll snag a few spoonfuls and put them in a bowl for a little pastina and cottage cheese snack.

The most important thing is to eat the *lokshen* (Yiddish for "noodles") right away. You could warm the pasta and cheese together in a pan so that the cheese gets slightly stringy, but I like the cool fresh curds with the hot pasta, a delicious contrast.

Cook the pasta in a large pot of rapidly boiling salted water; when al dente, drain and return to the hot pan.

Butter the pasta, season with salt and pepper, then toss with green onions. Toss with the cottage cheese, or serve in bowls with a spoonful of cottage cheese on each serving.

Eat right away.

12 ounces to 1 pound farfalle, fusilli, elbow macaroni, penne, rotelle, orecchiette, or cicatelli pasta

3 tablespoons unsalted butter, or ¼ cup extra-virgin olive oil, or as desired

Salt and freshly ground black pepper to taste

3 to 4 green onions (white and green parts) thinly sliced, or 3 cloves garlic, chopped

12 ounces to 1 pound cottage cheese, as desired

Gretchen's Buckwheat Soba with Cottage Cheese and Peas: My stepdaughter's favorite bowl of comfort. Choose a buckwheat pasta such as soba and add ½ to ⅔ cup of peas to the boiling water during the last minute or so that the pasta cooks. Drain and proceed with the recipe.

Farfalle con Ricotta: Prepare the farfalle as directed, but substitute ricotta for the cottage cheese, and use green onions, not garlic. Toss with a few tablespoons of freshly grated Parmesan or pecorino and serve.

Macaroni was made for soup—whether it is mouthfuls of the tiniest little dots of pastina, which give a simple broth substance, or chunky pasta, which adds texture to a hefty soup of earthy beans and vegetables.

Sometimes, cheese belongs deliciously in that soup pot, too. A big slice of meltable cheese, such as a youngish pecorino from Tuscany, laid at the bottom of a bowl and covered with a soup rich in vegetables, beans, and pasta is divine. Each bite contains a bit of fresh vegetable, a mouthful of tender bean, a satisfying chomp of macaroni, and a nubbin of melty, oozy cheese, which intermingles with the other ingredients. Or spoon into delicate broth, awash with a constellation of tiny stellini ("stars") or filled with semi di melone ("melon seeds") or orzo ("barley") pasta, the warm clear soup enriched with pungent Parmesan. Soup with macaroni and cheese has a zillion possibilities, and you can vary it through the seasons of the year, depending on what you find in your garden or at the produce market.

Then there is macaroni or pasta salad—a summertime treat in myriad flavors and guises. It is even tastier with a big hit of cheese: for example, cubes of sharp Cheddar in a Fourth of July macaroni salad, or slices of fresh mozzarella in a dish of pasta dressed with cilantro-mint chutney. And as for the salad of macaroni, fresh cheese, and romescu sauce, mmmm, don't even ask. Just wait for a nice sunny day, then go into the kitchen and make a bowlful.

Serves
4

Simple, classic broth, whether chicken, beef, or vegetable, is at its best with tiny pastina and a shower of nutty, pungent Parmesan cheese in every spoonful. Any additions to the bowl will be delicious, too—we have six variations in total. In fact, this recipe is nearly a complete book in itself! Once you're in the kitchen, simmering the stock and spooning in the pasta, no doubt you'll think of myriad combinations of macaroni and cheese for your soup pot.

12 ounces pastina, such as orzo, stellini, semi di melone, acini di pepe, alphabetti, or a similar small pasta

6 cups of chicken, beef, or vegetable broth, homemade or canned

Salt and freshly ground black pepper to taste

Freshly grated Parmesan for sprinkling

Cook the pasta in a large pot of rapidly boiling salted water until al dente; it will only take a few minutes as pastina are so tiny. Drain and rinse in cold water so they don't stick together. Set aside.

Heat the broth and season with salt and pepper as needed.

Spoon the pastina into bowls and ladle hot broth over them. Sprinkle extravagantly with Parmesan and enjoy.

Broccoli with Pastina Broth: Add a bunch of broccoli florets to the hot broth, along with 1 clove of garlic, chopped, and cook for 1 minute or so until the broccoli is crisp and bright green. Ladle the broth and broccoli into bowls and add a nice spoonful of cooked pastina and a generous sprinkling of Parmesan to each one. Enjoy!

Asparagus and Lime with Parmesan: Add bite-size lengths of asparagus to the bubbling broth along with 1 or 2 cloves of garlic, chopped. Ladle over the cooked orzo and blanket each bowlful of soup with freshly grated Parmesan, pecorino, or dry Jack cheese. Then squeeze a wedge of lime into each bowl.

Avgolemono from the Greek Island of Zakynthos:

This classic soup often contains freshly grated cheese in addition to its creamy egg-lemon broth, on the island of Zakynthos, due perhaps to its location—a few miles off the coast of Italy. Heat the chicken broth until bubbles form around the edge. Whisk 1 egg together with the juice of 1 to 2 lemons and several tablespoons of freshly grated Myzithra or pecorino cheese, then whisk in a ladleful of hot broth. Pour into the hot soup and warm through over medium heat, stirring, only until the liquid thickens slightly. Too much heat or cooking will scramble the eggs rather than form a creamy emulsion. Add several spoonfuls of cooked orzo to each bowl, and serve with extra grated pecorino for sprinkling.

Zucchini, Tiny Shells, Salsa, and Grated Pecorino:

Cook tiny shells or another very small pasta until al dente. Drain and rinse, and put a few spoonfuls in each bowl. Cook 2 zucchini, sliced, in the hot broth along with 1 or 2 cloves garlic, chopped. When the zucchini are tender, ladle the soup over the pasta in each bowl. Add a dab of some excellent salsa, preferably one with a nice hit of fresh cilantro, or sprinkle the soup with a little fresh cilantro you've chopped yourself. Sprinkle generously with pecorino.

Hortasoupa—Greek Greens, Pasta, and Cheese Soup:

The Greeks love the leafy greens of springtime, known as *horta;* hence, the name of this soup. Prepare the pastina and broth. Add about 2 cups of cooked, chopped greens, such as spinach or chard; the juice of ½ lemon; and 2 tablespoons of extra-virgin olive oil to the hot broth. Into each bowl place about 3 tablespoons of finely grated hard cheese, such as Sprinz, kefalotyri, pecorino, or Parmesan. Ladle in the hot soup and greens, add the pastina, and stir well so that the cheese blends with everything else in the bowl.

MINESTRONE AL PESTO CON FORMAGGIO

Vegetable Soup with Pesto and Cheese

Serves
4

Stir a spoonful of pesto into almost any Mediterranean vegetable and pasta soup, and you have your own version of a *minestrone al pesto*, a specialty of the Italian Riviera, from Genoa and Liguria. If you are across the border in France, on the Cote d'Azur, you may call it *soupe au pistou* (and leave out the prosciutto bone; *soupe au pistou* is resolutely vegetarian). The two versions are delectable siblings, lusty Mediterranean mélanges, rich with the scent of basil. My personal embellishment is a nice thick slab of cheese placed in the bottom of each bowl before I ladle in the hot soup. The cheese melts into soft strands and mouthfuls, making one of the coziest suppers imaginable.

Cook the pasta in a pot of rapidly boiling salted water until al dente; drain and set aside.

Lightly sauté the onion and garlic in the olive oil until softened, about 5 to 8 minutes. Add the broth and white wine, and the bone or prosciutto (if using). Cook for about 10 minutes, then add the cabbage, carrot, and tomatoes and continue to cook for about 30 minutes, or until the vegetables are very tender, especially the cabbage. Add the zucchini, spinach, green beans, and peas and cook for 10 to 15 minutes; then add the cannellini and thyme. Season with salt and pepper, if needed.

cont'd

4 ounces ditalini or small shells

1 onion, chopped

2 cloves garlic, chopped

2 tablespoons extra-virgin olive oil

1 quart vegetable or chicken broth, home-made or canned

1 cup dry white wine

1 prosciutto bone, or a few ounces diced prosciutto or another Italian cured meat (optional)

4 to 5 cabbage leaves, thinly sliced

1 carrot, thinly sliced

One 14-ounce can diced tomatoes, or about 2 cups diced fresh tomatoes

1 zucchini, sliced fairly thickly

cont'd

3 to 4 ounces fresh spinach leaves, coarsely chopped, or ½ cup cooked and drained frozen chopped spinach

Handful of green beans, cut into bite-size pieces

¼ cup fresh young peas, blanched, or frozen peas (no need to defrost)

½ cup cooked cannellini beans (canned are fine), drained

Large pinch of thyme, either fresh or dried

Salt and freshly ground black pepper to taste

About 6 ounces fontina, Jack, provolone, young (medium) Asiago, or cave-aged Gruyère cheese, cut into thick, slablike slices

½ cup pesto, homemade or store-bought

2 to 3 ounces Parmesan, pecorino, aged Asiago, or dry Jack cheese, grated

Into each bowl place a slab of cheese, then a big spoonful of the pasta and a dab of pesto. Ladle the hot soup over it all, and sprinkle the top with Parmesan. Serve at once!

PASTA CON PATATE

Pasta with Cheese and Potatoes from Old Napoli

Serves
4

Though *pasta con patate* is often made as a thick pasta course rather than a thick pasta-rich soup, the tomato-scented broth adds so much savor I can seldom resist making it this soupy way. Inhale the steamy fragrance, mmm, then spoon it up.

Pasta mista is an old tradition in some parts of Italy. You save the last bits of pasta from bags or boxes and mix them together. When you have enough, make a soup or a saucy pasta. For the best *pasta con patate,* choose artisanal pasta, as this type is substantial and chewy enough to stand up to the cooking. This recipe includes a little prosciutto or salami. For a vegetarian version, simply omit it and substitute vegetable broth for about half the water.

Lightly sauté the onion and half the garlic in the oil in a large heavy saucepan over medium-low heat until the onion has softened, 5 to 10 minutes. Add the potatoes, reduce the heat to low, and cook them with the onion and garlic, covered, for about 10 minutes. You don't want them to turn golden or fry, just to soften.

Add the tomatoes and remaining garlic and cook, stirring, until the tomatoes begin to soften and give up their juices, then add the tomato juice and water. Raise the heat and cook over medium-high heat, covered, until the potatoes are tender and beginning to fall apart. Season with the oregano, and salt and pepper.

Add the pasta to the hot, soupy potato mixture, along with the diced prosciutto, and cook over medium-high heat until the pasta is al dente. Stir occasionally, taking care that the mixture doesn't burn on the bottom, and add more water if needed.

When the pasta is just about cooked through, remove from heat, stir in the diced provolone, and cover the pot. Leave for 5 to 10 minutes, so the pasta finishes absorbing the liquid. Your mixture will be soupy, with bits of melty and slightly stringy cheese. Stir in the parsley. Ladle the soup into bowls, sprinkle with Parmesan, and serve.

1 onion, chopped

5 cloves garlic, chopped

3 tablespoons extra-virgin olive oil, plus extra for drizzling

3 to 4 potatoes (1 to 1½ pounds total), peeled and cut into 1 inch cubes

4 ripe tomatoes (about 1 pound), diced

½ cup tomato juice or *passata*, or to taste

1 quart water

Pinch of oregano

Salt and freshly ground black pepper to taste

8 ounces mixed sturdy pastas of similar sizes, such as shells, penne, radiatore, farfalle, ditali, gigli, and rotelle

2 ounces prosciutto or another Italian cured meat, diced or chopped

4 ounces cheese such as Neapolitan provola, provolone, or Jack, diced

3 tablespoons chopped parsley, preferably flat-leaf

About 2 ounces Parmesan cheese, grated

MARLENA'S MAHARAJAH MACARONI SALAD WITH GREEN CHUTNEY AND FRESH CHEESE

Serves
4

This salad is inspired by *paneer chalan,* an Indian dish of fresh cheese cooked in a sauce of cilantro, ginger, garlic, and mint. Though you might find the choice of oil strange—vegetable or extra-virgin olive—be assured that news of the health benefits of olive oil have reached the Indian subcontinent, and they now import it in enthusiastic quantities. Fresh cheese is eaten all over India. Called paneer, it's much like fresh mozzarella, which is also delicious in this salad. The milky, tender curd is the perfect counterpoint to the spunky, spicy green paste. Yum.

I'd serve nothing more than a bowl of ripe, perky cherry or grape tomatoes, to pick up and eat between bites of this pungent pasta salad. And for dessert, try lightly sugared strawberries or sliced plums sprinkled with rosewater to spoon over ice cream or thick Greek yogurt. This is what you want on a hot, sultry summer afternoon.

To make the Green Chutney: In a food processor, whirl the garlic and ginger to chop finely. Then add the chile and whirl to make a paste. Add the cilantro, mint, and vegetable oil, whirl, then add the yogurt and lemon juice and whirl again. Season with salt.

Cook the pasta in a large pot of rapidly boiling salted water until al dente. Drain and rinse in cold water. Toss the cool drained macaroni with the mozzarella cheese in a large bowl and then add green chutney.

GREEN CHUTNEY

6 cloves garlic

One 1-inch piece of ginger

½ to 1 fresh chile, chopped

1 cup fresh cilantro leaves

½ cup fresh mint leaves, or 2 heaping tablespoons dried mint

3 tablespoons vegetable or extra-virgin olive oil

3 tablespoons yogurt

Juice of 1 lemon or lime

Salt to taste

12 ounces short macaroni

6 to 8 ounces fresh, milky mozzarella cheese or Indian paneer, diced

AMALFI COAST ORECCHIETTE WITH LEMON, TANGY WHITE CHEESE, AND ARUGULA

Serves
4

Lemon, arugula, and tangy white cheese are scattered atop the chewy little pastas known as orecchiette, or "little ears," because of their shape and thickness. If you can't find orecchiette, choose farfalle, penne, or shells instead. Wild arugula—if you can get it—has even more flavor than the cultivated variety and a spicy bite to it. Make yourself a bowl of this refreshing cool pasta, then plan your trip to Napoli as you eat it.

You might like a nice pitcher of red wine with sliced juicy ripe peaches tossed in, as an *apperitivo* to sip before eating. Or switch the order, and make a bowlful of peaches sprinkled with sugar and splashed with a little red wine for a refreshing summer dessert.

1 large unwaxed lemon

12 ounces orecchiette

¼ cup extra-virgin olive oil

8 to 10 ounces Bulgarian, Israeli, or Greek feta cheese

Salt and freshly ground black pepper to taste

About 2 cups loosely packed arugula leaves (4 to 5 ounces)

Remove the zest from the lemon; I like to do this with a lemon zester as it is easiest and you get the most lemon flavor. It goes right to the bottom of the zest but leaves behind the white pith, which is bitter. A microplane works well, too, but a paring knife, which I do resort to occasionally, is the least satisfying in terms of lemon taste and ease. Whichever way you zest the lemon, set the shreds aside in a bowl. Squeeze the lemon juice into the bowl with the zest.

Cook the pasta in a large pot of rapidly boiling salted water for about 5 minutes. Continue cooking until it is tender, or remove from the heat and leave to sit in the hot water until it plumps up. The first method is quick; the second is slower, which may be an advantage if you're running behind in zesting the lemon or squeezing the juice, or if the phone rings and you get distracted.

Drain the al dente pasta and transfer to a large bowl. Add the lemon juice and zest and mix well. Toss in the olive oil and set aside for up to 2 hours before serving. When ready to serve, add the feta cheese, season with salt and pepper, and toss lightly. Serve, topped with the arugula leaves, at room temperature.

Serves
4

I do have a weakness for deliciously unfashionable mayo-driven mac and cheese salad. I mean, who needs refined taste when you've got a retro goodie like this: pickle relish! mayo! bright yellow mustard! But don't tell anyone I said so; I've got my image to think about.

This is a perfect Fourth of July and baseball-in-the-park picnic dish. Eat it alongside fat juicy burgers and "dawgs" hot off the grill.

Cook the pasta in a large pot of rapidly boiling salted water until al dente. Drain and rinse in cold water; leave it in the colander to continue to drain and cool.

When macaroni is dry and cool, place in a bowl with the onion and toss. Then add the ham, cheese, celery, and roasted pepper and toss again. Fold in the mayonnaise, mustard, and pickle relish. Season with paprika and salt and pepper and add a drop of vinegar. Taste and adjust the seasoning and chill until ready to serve.

8 ounces small elbow, ditalini, or another salad macaroni

1 onion, chopped

8 ounces ham or turkey ham, diced

8 ounces sharp, mature, full-flavored Cheddar type of cheese, diced

1 stalk celery, finely diced

1 roasted and peeled red or yellow bell pepper, diced or coarsely chopped, or an equivalent amount from a jar, drained

½ cup mayonnaise

1 tablespoon prepared yellow mustard

¼ cup pickle relish

½ teaspoon paprika, or to taste

Salt and freshly ground black pepper to taste

A few drops of vinegar

Spicy Catalan romesco sauce met Provençal rouille in my kitchen on a hot summer's night in Barcelona. Cilantro would definitely *not* lurk in either Catalonia or the Côte d'Azur, but it is emphatically delicious with the spicy dressing, tender macaroni, and bites of cheese.

Pimentón is smoked paprika, much like chipotle chile but without the heat.

Crisp fried baby artichokes might be nice to nibble alongside. Remove the tough outer leaves then slice thinly. Pan-fry in olive oil until browned in spots. Then drain on paper towels, sprinkle with chopped garlic, and serve.

Serves
4

Cook the pasta in a large pot of salted boiling water until al dente, and drain. Rinse with cold water and set aside in a large bowl. You want the pasta to be room temperature before you dress it.

In a food processor puree the garlic with the roasted red pepper, then add the chile powder, pimentón, mayonnaise, and cilantro and whirl until smooth. Slowly add the olive oil, then the tomato paste, sherry vinegar, and salt. Set aside.

The pasta may stick together as it cools, but never mind; it will all come apart in its dressing. Toss with the green onions, cherry tomatoes, and cheese. Add about half the dressing, toss well, then add the rest of the dressing and toss again.

Eat right away, or chill until ready to serve.

12 ounces small elbow macaroni

4 cloves garlic

1 roasted and peeled red bell pepper (from a jar is fine)

1½ to 2 teaspoons pure chile powder, such as ancho or New Mexico chile powder

1 teaspoon Spanish pimentón or sweet paprika combined with a few shakes of chipotle hot sauce, such as Tabasco or Bufala

¼ cup mayonnaise

½ cup fresh cilantro leaves

¼ cup extra-virgin olive oil

3 tablespoons tomato paste, or to taste

About 1 teaspoon sherry vinegar or red wine vinegar

Salt to taste

4 to 6 green onions (white and green parts), thinly sliced

12 cherry tomatoes, halved or quartered

6 ounces pecorino fresco, Hispanic panela, or queso fresco cheese, diced

Al dente pasta tossed with béchamel or crème fraîche, lots and lots of shredded cheese to melt into the dish alluringly, and voilà: macaroni and cheese cooked on top of the stove, moist, cheesy, and ready for you to fork it up happily.

You can always add a handful of herbs or a bit of chopped vegetables and a few bites of savory sausage or cured meats, and you can choose and combine your cheeses and pasta in endlessly delicious variations. This chapter romps through my own personal stove-top favorites, some with béchamel or crème fraîche, others with zesty tomato sauce. It all begins with a pot of boiling water, a package of pasta, and a wedge or two of cheese.

So put the water on to boil, shred the cheese, chop and stir, and get your big bowl ready for your mac and cheese!

DELICIOUSLY TRASHY MAC AND CHEESE WITH AN EXTRA HIT OF MUSTARD AND PICKLED JALAPEÑOS

Serves 4

Okay, we're starting off just slightly trashy, with evaporated milk. Sloshed into the elbow macaroni and the Cheddar, Jack, and Parmesan, it melts into a creamy sauce. Seriously, the evaporated milk lends a richness and hold-it-togetherness, with a touch of sweet milky flavor.

A sprinkling of pickled jalapeños at the end gives the dish a kick, and the sour cream gives it a tangy, creamy counterpoint. But don't try yellow or brown mustard in place of Dijon—the latter has the spicy, spunky quality that shakes up your mouth, and the former would just hijack the dish. (Cut back on the generous dose of both Dijon and pickled jalapeños, and you have a pretty classic stove-top mac and cheese.)

12 ounces small elbow macaroni

8 ounces evaporated milk

12 ounces sharp, mature Cheddar cheese, shredded

6 ounces Jack or a similar cheese, such as Gouda, shredded

⅓ to ½ cup freshly grated Parmesan or a similar hard grating cheese

1 or 2 shakes hot sauce, such as Tabasco

4 to 6 tablespoons sour cream or Greek yogurt

¼ cup Dijon mustard, or to taste

Salt and freshly ground black pepper to taste (optional)

⅛ to ¼ teaspoon paprika, or to taste

¼ cup pickled jalapeños, or as desired, chopped, sliced, or left whole

Cook the pasta in a large pot of rapidly boiling salted water until al dente and drain.

In a large heavy-bottomed saucepan, heat the evaporated milk over medium heat until bubbles form around the edge. Reduce the heat to low. Toss in the pasta, then sprinkle in the cheeses, in 3 or 4 batches, tossing the macaroni with the cheese after each addition so that the cheese melts. Add the hot sauce, sour cream, Dijon, and salt and pepper if needed. Warm through and sprinkle in the paprika.

Serve the mac and cheese with the chopped or sliced jalapeños scattered around the top, or serve with the whole jalapeños alongside.

You could even pour the complete dish, without the jalapeños, into a large deep baking dish and bake at 350°F for 30 to 35 minutes or until the top is crusty. But I think the appeal of this recipe is the speed with which you can throw it together.

ROASTED GREEN CHILE AND TOMATILLO
MAC AND CHEESE

Serves
4

I love the combination of feisty chile, tangy green tomatillo, and lots of garlic and cilantro, all bound up with melty cheese and just enough smooth sour cream, laban (strained yogurt cheese), or Greek yogurt to keep it all together.

Alongside, how about a salad of radishes, avocado, tomato, a few shreds of romaine, and lots of green onion dressed in lime juice and olive oil?

Cut the chile in half and remove the seeds. Chop one of the chile halves and place in a bowl. Place the other chile half, skin side down, directly over a low flame if you have gas burners, or place it under the broiler, skin side up. Roast the chile until it chars in spots, moving it around for even scorching. Remove from the heat, put in a plastic bag or bowl, and either knot the bag or cover the bowl tightly with plastic wrap. When cool enough to handle, remove the charred skin. Alternatively, to save time, rinse the hot chile under cold water and peel off as much of the scorched skin as you can. Thinly slice the roasted chile and add to it as much of the chopped raw chile as you like; this will depend on both your affection for chile heat and the heat of the chile itself—some are milder, some hotter. I'd start with a small amount of the chopped raw chile and add more to taste. Into the bowl of the mixed raw and roasted chiles, add the green onions, garlic, and cilantro. Set aside.

cont'd

1 Anaheim or poblano chile

3 to 5 green onions (white and green parts), thinly sliced

3 cloves garlic, chopped

½ bunch cilantro, coarsely chopped

12 ounces ditalini, seashell, penne, small rigatoni, rotelle, or radiatore pasta

¼ cup sour cream, Greek yogurt, laban (strained yogurt cheese), or crème fraîche

8 ounces mature Cheddar or another sharp cheese, shredded

4 ounces Lancashire, Wensleydale, fresh pecorino, semi secco, or queso fresco cheese, crumbled

4 ounces pecorino, dry Jack, or aged Asiago cheese, shredded or grated

Drizzle of extra-virgin olive oil

4 to 5 tablespoons green tomatillo salsa

1 lime, cut into wedges

Cook the pasta in a large pot of rapidly boiling salted water until al dente. Drain, reserving ½ cup or so of the cooking water.

Return the pasta to the pot, and toss with the sour cream and about a third of the cheeses, sprinkled evenly over the top and then carefully tossed with the pasta. If you are too cavalier when adding a large amount of grated cheese without a big sauce, it can clump together disastrously. Repeat with half of the remaining cheese mixture, then add a drizzle of olive oil and the salsa, and toss again with the rest of the cheese and the reserved chile mixture. If the dish seems dry, add a few tablespoons of the reserved cooking water or as much as you need. Toss over the heat a moment or two, then pour into the serving bowl.

Serve with lime wedges to squeeze in as desired, and extra salsa and/or chopped raw chile for those who dare.

LEAH'S HOMEY GREEK MACARONI AND CHEESE

Serves
4

Make this on a cold Saturday night. Eat it from a big bowl, sitting on the couch in your stocking feet—with your child, husband, best friend, cat, or by yourself.

I'm not sure how I started making this dish, but it was probably based on what our pantry had to offer as well as my memories of Greek island life. The more immediate inspirations were hungry mother (me) and equally hungry daughter (the Leah of the recipe title). The vegetable juice would have been a pantry substitute for the diced tomato I used in Greece (but we came to love the vegetable juice even more). I also added more cheese than Greek islanders would dream of. A comfort dish extraordinaire.

We liked to eat crunchy raw vegetables to start with: radishes, celery, and cucumbers. And we munched on cherry tomatoes, too, biting down on them, one at a time, the little tomatoes exploding in our mouths! Afterward we sometimes made chocolate-roasted bananas. It's quite simple: Make a slit on one side of an unpeeled banana, stick in as many slices of dark chocolate as will fit, put on a baking sheet, chocolate side up, and bake at 400°F for about 10 minutes, or long enough to melt the chocolate. Eat the smooshy hot banana and chocolate with a spoon directly from the banana skin, and you won't even need to wash up.

Lightly sauté the garlic in the olive oil in a heavy saucepan over medium heat. Sprinkle with the flour, stir to cook through, then remove from heat. Add the hot milk all at once, then stir with a wooden spoon, pressing any lumps against the side of the pan to dissolve them. (You can make the sauce with cold milk if you are feeling lazy. You'll have more lumps, but wielding your wooden spoon or balloon whisk should get rid of the main offenders, and a few lumps here and there will get lost in the sauce, pasta, and melted cheese.) Return the sauce to the stove and cook, stirring with a wooden spoon, until the mixture thickens, about 5 to 7 minutes. Add the vegetable juice and continue simmering until the sauce thickens once again and the flavors concentrate. Season with cinnamon, allspice, and oregano.

cont'd

2 cloves garlic, chopped

2 tablespoons olive oil or unsalted butter

2 tablespoons flour

2 cups hot, but not boiling, milk (low-fat is fine)

1 cup tomato and mixed vegetable juice, such as V8

⅛ teaspoon ground cinnamon, or to taste

⅛ teaspoon ground allspice or cloves, or to taste

¼ teaspoon dried oregano leaves, or to taste, crumbled between your fingers

cont'd

12 to 16 ounces short fat pasta, such as shells, elbows, penne, or rotelle

12 ounces kasseri, kefalotyri, youngish pecorino, Jack, or provolone, or any combination of these or similar cheeses, cut into ½-inch dice

Salt and freshly ground black pepper to taste

Sharp hard grating cheese, such as pecorini, dry Jack, or Parmesan, grated

You will probably need more than is suggested—I find that the dish tastes best when it has more cinnamon and allspice than seems reasonable.

Cook the pasta in a large pot of rapidly boiling salted water until al dente, then drain.

Return the hot pasta to the pan, add the sauce, and place over low heat. Toss together, then add the cheese and toss it with all the pasta and sauce. Season with salt and pepper.

Serve right away, sprinkled with the hard grating cheese.

SEXY MAYOR OF ROME CARBONARA

Serves
4

Franco Rutelli, the sexy mayor of Rome in the mid-1990s, had a cocktail party in London. Lucky me, I was on the guest list. As Mayor Rutelli made his way through the group, smiling charmingly, he held my offered hand just a moment too long, long enough to melt my poise, cause my heart to beat rather loudly, and make me look for the nearest chair. I looked around me. All of the other chairs were taken with women similarly affected.

The cocktail hour passed and we were well into the hour for pasta. I was sitting and regrouping my strength, when out came a big platter. Heaped onto a homey tray, possibly of the disposable sort, was a delicious mountain of Rome's favorite pasta—alla carbonara. Everyone gathered around to help him- or herself while it was still hot and saucy. It was so delicious that few among us could restrain ourselves from unabashed greediness.

The pasta we ate was actually a variation of the famous carbonara, which is traditionally tossed with browned pancetta or bacon, Parmesan, and raw eggs. The hot pasta cooks the raw egg and cheese into a soft, clinging sauce. Our pasta was slightly more refined, with strips of lean prosciutto in place of the chunkier pancetta or bacon. Though the recipe calls for fettuccine, almost any shape of sturdy pasta is terrific, especially penne or chewy, barely al dente spaghetti; delicate pasta such as vermicelli or *capelli d'angelo* are not. You can make your carbonara completely vegetarian if you like: simply omit the meaty bits altogether and add a handful of vegetables to the pasta toward the end of its cooking time—diced zucchini, tiny peas, asparagus tips, or chopped red or yellow bell pepper.

1 large onion, chopped

3 to 4 tablespoons unsalted butter

½ cup dry white wine

½ cup chicken or vegetable broth, homemade or canned

4 ounces prosciutto, cut into strips

2 eggs, lightly beaten

About 3 ounces Parmesan cheese, grated, plus extra for serving

In a large heavy-bottomed sauté pan, lightly sauté the onion in the butter over medium heat until it has softened and turned golden in color, then add the white wine and boil down until only a few spoonfuls remain. Add the broth and cook over high heat for several minutes, or until it, too, is slightly reduced. Remove from the heat and stir in the prosciutto.

In a medium bowl mix the eggs with the Parmesan and hard cheese, season with salt and pepper, and set aside.

About 1 ounce hard cheese, such as Sprinz or pecorino, grated or shredded

Salt and freshly ground black pepper to taste

1 pound fresh fettuccine or 12 ounces dried pasta, such as spaghetti or penne

Cook the pasta in a large pot of rapidly boiling salted water until just al dente. Drain, reserving about ¼ cup of the cooking water.

Toss the hot pasta with the egg-and-cheese mixture, mixing well to coat each strand evenly; it will cook lightly with the heat of the pasta. Next, toss the pasta with the onion and reduced broth. Return to the heat for a moment or two, adding and tossing with enough of the reserved cooking water to bring together the various ingredients into a lovely, clinging sauce.

Serve right away, with additional Parmesan for grating over each bowl individually.

BUCKWHEAT PASTA
WITH **CRAB, PEAS,** AND **MASCARPONE**

Serves
4

If it's crab season, get yourself to the seashore in time to meet the returning fishermen. This dish of earthy buckwheat pasta, rich creamy mascarpone, tiny fresh peas, and sweet briny crabmeat is the one to make now.

Japanese soba and Italian pizzoccheri are both delicious buckwheat pasta. Soba is delicate and pizzoccheri is robust; either is delicious in this dish. If you are catching the crabs yourself, remember that you want them to remain alive and wriggling. Once a crab has been out of water for a while and stops moving, it is too late to use it because deterioration sets in quickly. The crab must be cooked when still perky. It is a brutal task, indeed. For the faint-hearted (myself emphatically included), it is easiest to buy the crabs already cooked. And truth be known, it's easier still to buy the meat already pried out of the shells.

3 to 5 tablespoons unsalted butter

2 cloves garlic, chopped

8 to 12 ounces cooked fresh white crabmeat, picked over for tiny bits of shell and cartilage

1 cup small fresh or frozen peas

12 ounces buckwheat soba or pizzoccheri

1 cup mascarpone cheese or heavy cream

A few drops of fresh lemon juice

2 to 3 ounces Parmesan, aged Asiago, or dry Jack, grated, plus extra for serving

In a large sauté or frying pan, melt the butter over medium-low heat, then add the garlic and warm through, but do not brown. Stir in the crabmeat and warm in the garlic butter, then add the peas, cover, and set aside.

Cook the pasta in a large pot of rapidly boiling salted water until al dente. Drain gently (buckwheat pasta tends to fall apart easily), reserving a few tablespoons or so of the cooking liquid.

Toss the drained pasta in the pan with the garlicky crab. Add the mascarpone in dollops all over the pasta and toss it all together. Add a few drops of lemon juice to balance the cream's richness, toss in the grated cheese, and add a few tablespoons of the reserved cooking water, if needed.

Serve immediately, and pass extra grated cheese at the table.

Lobster and Pea Tagliatelle: Substitute lobster meat for the crab, and a delicate fresh tagliatelle or fettuccine instead of the buckwheat pasta. Serve sprinkled with chopped fresh chervil.

MACARONI WITH MOROCCAN-SPICED BUTTER AND SHREDDED GOAT OR SHEEP CHEESE

Serves
4

This is not a melty macaroni and cheese. Instead, the macaroni is lavished with a spicy butter, then blanketed with shavings of pungent goat or sheep cheese. The dish is delicious eaten with friends, but also nice spooned up on a solitary evening.

I'd nibble a few North African–inspired vegetable appetizers to start with: steamed carrots tossed with cumin, cinnamon, garlic, olive oil, and lemon juice; tomatoes and onion with shreds of preserved lemon; and boiled potatoes with capers, garlic, olive oil and lemon juice.

1 large dried mild red chile, such as ancho or New Mexico, ground in a clean coffee grinder; or about 2 teaspoons pure mild red chile powder, such as ancho or New Mexico, or to taste

5 to 8 green onions (white and green parts), thinly sliced

3 to 5 cloves garlic, crushed

1 tablespoon paprika

1 tablespoon ground cumin

1 teaspoon ground coriander

2 tablespoons chopped fresh parsley

2 tablespoons chopped fresh mint

3 to 4 tablespoons chopped fresh cilantro

½ cup (1 stick) unsalted butter at room temperature

¼ to ½ teaspoon fresh lemon or lime juice

Salt to taste

12 ounces small tubular pasta or farfalline (small butterflies), or smallish to medium rigatoni

6 ounces hard grating goat or sheep cheese, such as pecorino, crottin, or Myzithra, shaved or coarsely shredded

Combine the red chile powder with the green onions, garlic, paprika, cumin, coriander, parsley, mint, and cilantro in a food processor and whirl together. Add the butter in chunks and whirl until it all forms a smooth, creamy mixture. Add the lemon juice and season with salt. Set aside. If storing for over an hour, refrigerate.

Cook the pasta in a large pot of rapidly boiling salted water until al dente. Drain, saving about ¼ cup of the cooking liquid.

Toss the hot macaroni with as much of the butter as desired. (Any leftover butter is delicious melted onto grilled chicken, fish, or burgers.) Sprinkle about half the cheese on the hot macaroni and toss gently. Then serve in bowls with the remaining cheese sprinkled on top.

Eat right away!

MACARONI WITH WHITE TRUFFLE BUTTER AND GRATED PECORINO

Serves
4

Make only as much as you want to eat now, as this pales in flavor and aroma once the genie— in this case, the truffle oil—is out of the bottle. When adding it to the butter and garlic, keep shaking that arm until you've dribbled in enough oil to get the flavor you want. Truffle oils have different levels of scent and flavor, so an exact amount is not specified.

6 tablespoons unsalted butter at room temperature

2 cloves garlic, crushed

Several very generous shakes of white truffle oil

12 ounces macaroni

4 to 6 ounces pecorino cheese, grated

Combine the butter with the garlic and truffle oil in a large bowl. Mix well, cover, and set aside.

Cook the pasta in a large pot of rapidly boiling salted water and drain.

Toss the macaroni with the truffle butter and as much pecorino cheese as desired.

NOODLES WITH GREEN PARSLEY–GARLIC BUTTER

Garlic-parsley butter is what makes escargots delicious and transforms a simple grilled steak into an elegant entree. Tossed with hot pasta and a sprinkling of grated cheese it, makes a side dish par excellence, a lovely bed for grilled fish, or warming bowl of noodles to eat on its own.

Combine the butter with the parsley and garlic in a large bowl and mix well. Season with salt and pepper and add the lemon juice.

Boil the pasta in a large pot of rapidly boiling salted water until al dente. Drain and toss with parsley butter, then sprinkle with Emmenthal and Parmesan and toss to mix well.

Serves 4

6 tablespoons unsalted butter at room temperature

3 tablespoons finely chopped parsley

3 to 4 cloves garlic, finely chopped

Salt and freshly ground black pepper to taste

¼ teaspoon fresh lemon juice

12 ounces egg or spinach noodles

4 ounces Emmenthal or cave-aged Gruyère, shredded

3 ounces Parmesan, pecorino, or aged Asiago, grated

MACARONI WITH SHALLOT-CHIVE BUTTER AND YOUNG FRESH GOAT CHEESE

Serves
4

Chewy tender macaroni, lightly buttered and studded with shallots and chives—so utterly delicious topped with a snowy billow of fresh goat cheese.

If you prefer, fresh cow's milk cheese is delicious too: Cowgirl Creamery's fromage blanc is a personal favorite, or any fromage frais or fromage blanc.

In a large bowl, combine the butter with the shallot and chives. Mix well, then season with salt and pepper and add the lemon juice.

Cook the pasta in a large pot of rapidly boiling salted water until al dente. Drain, and toss the hot macaroni with the shallot-chive butter. Serve each bowlful with a big dollop of fresh goat cheese for each diner to mix in.

6 tablespoons unsalted butter at room temperature

1 shallot, chopped

2 tablespoons chopped fresh chives

Salt and freshly ground black pepper to taste

A few drops of fresh lemon juice

12 ounces elbow macaroni, penne, or farfalle

3 to 4 ounces mild, creamy goat cheese, such as Montrachet or a log from California, Israel, or Wales

PENNE with ZUCCHINI, RICOTTA, and WALNUTS

Serves
4

Enjoy hot pasta, drifts of milky fresh ricotta, and a blanketing of pungent, salty Parmesan or pecorino with nearly any vegetable that is in season at the moment. Though I love zucchini most of all, their delicate blossoms are also good, as are golden zucchini or summer squash, young fava beans, crisp green Romano beans, broccoli, leafy chard, or roasted red or yellow bell peppers. Walnuts give this Tuscan specialty a crunchy, earthy edge. A chunky spinach pasta is terrific with the ricotta and nuts in this dish, instead of the penne.

Cook the pasta in a big pot of rapidly boiling salted water for 5 minutes, or until halfway to al dente; add the zucchini and continue cooking until al dente. Drain and reserve about 1/4 cup of the cooking water.

Return the hot pasta and zucchini to the pan and toss with the garlic, olive oil, ricotta and pecorino cheeses, walnuts, and thyme. Toss in a few spoonfuls of the cooking water and season with salt and pepper. Serve right away.

Pasta with Broccoli, Ricotta, and Walnuts:
Substitute broccoli, cut into bite-size florets, for the zucchini, and add a pinch of red pepper flakes to the oil. If you like, orecchiette are always good with broccoli.

Pasta with Zucchini, Walnuts, and Goat Cheese:
Substitute fresh mild goat cheese for the ricotta.

Spicy Pasta with Swiss Chard and Fresh Cheese:
Substitute panfried sliced Swiss chard leaves for the zucchini and add a pinch of red pepper flakes to the oil.

Pasta with Roasted Red Peppers, Pine Nuts, and Ricotta: Replace the zucchini with about 2 roasted, peeled, and sliced red peppers (from a jar is fine), and substitute pine nuts for the walnuts.

14 ounces penne or another chunky pasta, such as spinach fusilli

3 to 4 zucchini, sliced

3 cloves garlic, chopped

¼ cup extra-virgin olive oil

3 to 4 ounces ricotta cheese

About ½ cup freshly grated aged pecorino, dry Jack, aged Asiago cheese, or Parmesan

½ cup walnut pieces

1 to 2 teaspoons fresh thyme leaves

Salt and freshly ground black pepper to taste

CICATELLI with PUMPKIN and SAGE

Serves
4

Here is a classic combination of earthy, sweet pumpkin or hubbard, kabocha, or butternut squash; bitter, herbaceous sage; chewy pasta; and rich cheese. While pumpkin and hubbard and winter squash need to be peeled, the dark green peel on kabocha may be eaten. The cicatelli are like fat closed shells, a bit like the Sardinian malloreddus pasta. If you can't locate either of them, gemelli—"twin" pasta lengths twisting around each other—are delish. A shredding of prosciutto or *jamon serrano* adds a salty, refined edge.

For dessert, you'll want a bright fruit granita or deep, dark chocolate gelato, drizzled with grappa or amaretto—no question about it.

1 pound pumpkin, hubbard, or butternut squash, peeled or kabocha (unpeeled, if desired), cut into bite-size pieces (about ¾ inch in size)

4 tablespoons unsalted butter or extra-virgin olive oil

8 to 10 young flavorful sage leaves, thinly sliced

6 cloves garlic, chopped

8 ounces cicatelli, malloreddus, gemelli, or another chewy pasta

3 to 5 tablespoons crème fraîche, or as desired

6 ounces fontina or another white flavorful cheese, shredded

4 to 6 tablespoons freshly grated aged Asiago or Parmesan cheese

Salt and freshly ground black pepper to taste

4 ounces prosciutto or Serrano ham, cut into strips or diced

Lightly sauté the pumpkin in 3 tablespoons of the butter or oil over medium-low heat until it browns lightly in spots and becomes tender, but not mushy. About halfway through the cooking time, add half the sage and garlic. Set aside.

Cook the pasta in a large pot of rapidly boiling salted water until al dente. Drain and save about ¼ cup of the cooking liquid.

Toss the hot pasta with the hot sautéed pumpkin, and spoon in the crème fraîche and half the cheese. Toss together over a medium-low heat on the stove with a few spoonfuls of the cooking liquid. Add the rest of the cheese, toss with the pasta, then toss in the remaining 1 tablespoon butter, sage, and garlic and season with salt and pepper.

Serve immediately, sprinkled with the prosciutto.

CALYPSO-RONI

Serves
4

A friend once went to one of the Caribbean islands and came back quite supple from dancing under that little limbo stick, and also quite smitten with a dish of macaroni and meaty tomato sauce with melted cheese on top. This resembles the dish she described, though I confess to adding the cilantro. The result: perfection!

Slice up a ripe, juicy mango or papaya for dessert and douse with lime juice. And if you are feeling a bit more indulgent, add a scoop each of mango sorbet and vanilla ice cream to each serving.

12 ounces lean ground beef or ground sirloin

2 onions, chopped

8 ounces bacon, cut into ¼- to ½-inch pieces

1 bay leaf

2 teaspoons chopped fresh thyme, or ¼ to ½ teaspoon dried thyme, crumbled between the fingers

¼ teaspoon allspice

1 cup dry white wine

2 cups diced tomatoes, fresh or canned

3 tablespoons tomato paste, or to taste

Salt and freshly ground black pepper to taste

12 ounces small rigatoni or another small to medium tubular pasta

10 to 12 ounces mild or sharp Cheddar cheese, or a combination of the two, cut into ⅛- to ¼-inch slices

A few shakes hot sauce, such as a Caribbean one, or to taste

3 to 4 tablespoons chopped fresh cilantro

Preheat the broiler.

Brown the ground meat with the onions and bacon in a heavy nonstick frying pan over medium heat until lightly browned; break it up with a spatula as it cooks and browns.

Add the bay leaf, thyme, allspice, and wine and bring to a boil. Continue cooking over medium-high heat until the liquid reduces by about half. Add the tomatoes and tomato paste and simmer for 5 minutes or so. Taste for salt and season with pepper. Cover and set aside.

Cook the pasta in a large pot of rapidly boiling salted water until al dente.

Add the rigatoni to the sauce and heat them together. Tip the mixture into a large shallow baking dish, top with the cheese, and pop under the broiler for about 5 minutes, or until the cheese melts and lightly browns.

Add a few shakes of hot sauce and a sprinkling of cilantro and serve.

MEDITERRANEAN MACARONI MADNESS

Chopped roasted bell peppers tossed with pungent Greek island or Italian countryside cheeses, pasta shells, a whiff of garlic and basil, and a scattering of pine nuts make up this delicious and simple bowl of pasta.

Sliced cucumber makes a tasty accompaniment, or maybe a plate of baby pea shoots to pick up with your fingers.

Roast each bell pepper directly over a low flame if you have gas burners, turning every so often so that the pepper chars and blisters all over. Alternatively, you may arrange the peppers on a baking sheet or in a pan and place them under the broiler until they are charred and blistered, turning every so often for even browning. Put the roasted peppers in a bowl and cover tightly with plastic wrap. Leave for about 30 minutes, then peel. The skin should slip off easily. If you do not wish to wait, peel and rinse under cold water. Remove the stems and seeds, and slice the pepper flesh into strips about ¼-inch wide and 2-inches long.

Combine the peppers, tomatoes, garlic, ricotta, kefalotyri, and black pepper in a large bowl.

Cook the pasta in a large pot of rapidly boiling salted water until it is al dente and drain.

Spoon about a third of the cheese mixture into the hot pot, add the pasta, and toss together over very low heat, adding more and more of the cheese mixture and tossing continually, until the mixture is hot and melty. Liquid from the vegetables will collect at the bottom of the pot; this makes a lovely light sauce. But don't cook for too long as the cheese will curdle and you'll have too much liquid! Toss in the basil, pine nuts, and olive oil and serve immediately.

1 medium to large red bell pepper

1 medium to large yellow bell pepper

3 ripe tomatoes, cut into ⅛- to ¼-inch dice

3 cloves garlic, chopped

5 to 6 ounces ricotta, fromage frais, fromage blanc, or Greek galatyri cheese

12 ounces kefalotyri, Asiago, Italian fontina, or youngish, pungent pecorino cheese, shredded

Freshly ground black pepper to taste

12 to 14 ounces shells, elbow macaroni, or a similar pasta

5 to 6 tablespoons finely shredded fresh basil

¼ cup pine nuts

2 tablespoons extra-virgin olive oil

This is macaroni and cheese at its most alluringly classic: Layer slightly undercooked macaroni with cheese in a casserole, top with a handful of crumbs, then bake to get it crispy-topped and sizzling.

But don't stop there: Mix the pasta with béchamel for creaminess, or tomato sauce for zest, add a handful of vegetables, a sprinkling of fresh herbs, and a scattering of browned meats or briny fish (think tuna-noodle casserole).

Béchamel can be made ahead of time and kept, covered, for about 3 days in the refrigerator. Similarly, the pasta can be cooked ahead earlier in the day, though its texture will suffer from refrigeration.

The possibilities for pasta and cheese combinations are nearly endless. Aim a dart at your world map and chances are, wherever it lands you will find a cheese and a pasta that will be good when layered and baked together—so good, they will inspire a deep sigh of happiness when you plunge your fork in.

Do remember, though, when you are cooking pasta that will be baked, to undercook it slightly. Drain it when it is about three quarters of the way done, or even sooner. It will continue to cook in the oven between the sauce and the cheese.

And just a reminder: While macaroni and cheese is delicious freshly baked, it's wonderful the next day, too. You can eat leftover macaroni and cheese cold, cut into slabs, like a Caribbean macaroni pie (page 104). Or reheat baked macaroni and cheese in a nonstick pan with a few tablespoons of water, letting it melt into a delicious mass of soft macaroni and gooey cheese.

YANKEE DOODLE DANDY
BAKED MACARONI AND CHEESE

This is quintessential American macaroni and cheese, quite close to the classic British version that so beguiled Mrs. Raffald in her cookery book of the late 1700s, and even Richard II's royal court. Like the British dish, it is made with béchamel sauce and Cheddar. Our American mac and cheese tends to include paprika, bay leaf, and powdered or prepared mustard, while the British one sticks with a whiff of mace and a nip of British mustard strong enough to bring a tear to even the toughest man's eye.

Though many classic mac and cheese recipes suggest sautéing the onion before adding it, I think the zippiness of raw onion tastes best in this dish, and of course is easier. Oh, yes, the other thing I add—perhaps no surprise to those who know me—is a little chopped garlic.

This can be made on the stove top instead of baked, by the way, something I often do if I'm in a hurry or if the weather is warm and I'm not up for turning on the oven and heating the kitchen. To make this on the stove top, simply cook the pasta for a slightly longer time, until al dente, toss with the sauce and cheese, and serve it up directly from the pot.

Serves
4

Cook the pasta in a pot of rapidly boiling salted water until not quite tender—just shy of al dente. Drain and set aside.

Preheat the oven to 375°F.

Melt 3 tablespoons of the butter in a heavy nonstick saucepan and sprinkle with the flour. Cook for a minute or two, then stir with a wooden spoon. Remove from the heat and add the milk all at once, along with the bay leaf. Cook, stirring, over medium-high heat until the sauce thickens, about 5 to 7 minutes. If there are any lumps, remove the bay leaf and whisk with a wire whisk or whirl in the food processor. Remove from the heat and season with the salt and pepper, paprika, and dry mustard.

cont'd

12 ounces large elbow macaroni, farfalle (butterfly- or bowtie-shaped pasta) or conchiglie (shells)

3 tablespoons unsalted butter or 1 ½ tablespoons butter plus 1 ½ tablespoons extra-virgin olive oil

3 tablespoons flour

3 cups hot, but not boiling, milk (low-fat is fine)

1 bay leaf

cont'd

Salt and freshly ground black pepper to taste

½ teaspoon paprika

1 tablespoon dry mustard

14 ounces sharp Cheddar cheese, shredded

6 ounces mild white meltable cheese, such as Jack, Gouda, or kasseri, shredded

3 ounces sharp blue cheese, crumbled

1 cup dry breadcrumbs, either homemade or unseasoned store-bought (optional)

½ onion, finely chopped

1 clove garlic, chopped (optional)

⅓ to ½ cup freshly grated Parmesan, pecorino, or Sprinz cheese

Reserve 3 ounces of the Chedder, 3 ounces of the Jack, and 2 tablespoons of the Parmesan. Remove the bay leaf from the sauce if you haven't already, then stir in the remaining Cheddar, Jack cheese, and blue cheese and set aside.

If using breadcrumbs, in a small frying pan, heat the remaining 3 tablespoons of the butter or the olive oil and combine it with the breadcrumbs. Set aside.

In the bottom of a 1½-quart baking dish with 4-inch sides, sprinkle 1 or 2 tablespoons of the reserved cheese. Add the onion and garlic to the cheese sauce.

Layer a third of the macaroni in the bottom of the baking dish, top with a third of the cheese sauce, and repeat the layers two more times, ending with the cheese sauce. Sprinkle with the remaining shredded cheeses, then with the Parmesan cheese, and finally with the breadcrumbs, if using. Bake for 20 to 25 minutes, or until the top is crispy and browned in spots.

Eat hot!

Macaroni and Broccoli and Cheese: This is really, really good. The strong flavor of the broccoli is delish with the tangy and rich cheese sauce. It's like a retro chicken divan without the chicken. Add a layer or two of blanched broccoli florets as you assemble the casserole. End with a layer of broccoli before you top with the cheese and crumbs. Bake as directed.

TUNA-NOODLE CASSEROLE

Serves
4 to 6

Darryl Corti, owner of Sacramento's Corti Brothers, purveyors of the most delicious things on this planet, and I share a guilty little secret. We both love tuna, and not just the trendy grilled, seared, and sushi tuna so popular these days, but in our heart of hearts, we cherish canned tuna. (Darryl sells the most gorgeous varieties of canned tuna!) And it doesn't stop there: We both dote on tuna-noodle casserole, too. Of course, it must be wonderful tuna-noodle casserole made with homemade béchamel, tuna of delicious excellence, tender noodles, and sharp, tasty cheese.

We have long talked of holding a tuna-noodle casserole extravaganza, and one of these days we'll organize it. In the meantime, this is my favorite version, which I'll be bringing to the party; it has mushrooms and peas.

Preheat the oven to 375°F.

In a large, heavy nonstick saucepan, melt 4 tablespoons of the butter over medium-low heat. Add the onion and cook until it softens; add the mushrooms and raise the heat slightly to cook them through. Sprinkle the onion and mushrooms with flour, stir for a few minutes to cook out the flavor of the flour, add the dried porcini to the pot, and remove from the heat. Stir in the broth with a wooden spoon and keep stirring to break up any floury lumps and make a smoothish sauce. Stir in the milk and return to the stove.

Cook the sauce over medium-high heat, stirring, for about 7 to 10 minutes, or until it thickens. If there are any floury lumps, whisk the sauce briefly with a wire whisk. Remove from the heat and season with the nutmeg and salt and pepper. Set the sauce aside.

cont'd

6 tablespoons unsalted butter, plus extra for buttering the pan

1 medium onion, chopped

1 cup thinly sliced mushrooms

¼ cup flour

½ ounce (1 or 2 generous pinches) dry porcini mushrooms, broken into small pieces

1 cup chicken or vegetable broth, homemade or canned

2 cups hot, but not boiling, milk (low-fat is fine)

cont'd

A grating of fresh nutmeg

Salt and freshly ground black, white, or
cayenne pepper to taste

12 ounces wide noodles, such as egg noodles

6 ounces sharp Cheddar or Cheddar type of
cheese, shredded

Two 6-ounce cans good-quality tuna, packed
in oil or water, drained

½ to ¾ cup fresh peas, blanched, or frozen
peas, defrosted

3 tablespoons chopped fresh parsley

3 to 4 tablespoons dry breadcrumbs

Cook the pasta in a large pot of rapidly boiling salted
water until it is not quite al dente, as it will cook further
in the oven, and drain.

In a buttered large shallow pan, in layers, add a quarter of
the sauce, a quarter of the cheese, and a third of the tuna,
peas, and noodles. Repeat the layers two more times, and
then end with a layer of sauce and a layer of cheese. Sprinkle
with the parsley and crumbs, then dot with the remaining
2 tablespoons of butter.

Bake the casserole until bubbly, lightly browned, and crisped
in spots, about 30 minutes. Serve right away.

Macaroni and Cheese Under the Sea: Omit the tuna,
and add a selection of mixed shellfish, such as shrimp,
diced scallops, nuggets of lobster or crab, and rings of squid.
Substitute a mild white cheese such as Jack, fontina,
provolone, or Emmenthaler for the sharp Cheddar. Serve
sprinkled with the delicious, grassy, utterly French herb,
chervil. Or, for a decidedly "Newberg-ish" fifties flavor, add
a tablespoon or two of dry sherry to the simmering sauce
before adding it to the casserole.

HAPPINESS MACARONI WITH HAM, PEAS, AND MANY CHEESES

Serves
4

The truth: I was whipping this up, happy as can be (I'm always happy when I making macaroni and cheese, and this one was a "freewheeling fling open the fridge door and see what we have"). Then it hit me. I should write a book about macaroni and cheese! And when we sat down to eat this, it was sooo good, I thought, forget "should," I *must* write a book about macaroni and cheese!

For dessert? Crisp cookies such as gingersnaps or biscotti, with a glass of Vin Santo to dip into.

Preheat the oven to 375°F.

Melt the butter in a heavy nonstick saucepan over medium-low heat. Sprinkle in the flour and cook for a moment or two. Remove from the heat and add the milk all at once, stirring with a wooden spoon. Return to the stove and, over a medium-high heat, cook, stirring, until the sauce thickens, about 5 to 7 minutes. Stir in the salt, cayenne, and nutmeg. If there are a few lumps, whisk them with a wire whisk. If there are still a few lumps, leave them. With all the other goodies they won't be noticeable.

Remove the sauce from the stove and add the ham, peas, cottage cheese, and feta cheese, and mix well. Stir in the shredded Gruyère and half the Parmesan. Set aside.

Cook the pasta in a large pot of rapidly boiling salted water until almost al dente. Drain well, then toss with the sauce, ham, peas, and cheese mixture.

Pour the mixture into a 1½- to 2-quart baking dish with 4-inch sides and sprinkle with the remaining Parmesan. Bake for 15 to 20 minutes, or until the top is lightly browned in spots. Serve right away.

2 tablespoons unsalted butter

2 tablespoons flour

2 cups hot, but not boiling, milk (low-fat is fine), plus extra if needed

Salt and cayenne pepper to taste

A grating of fresh nutmeg, or to taste

4 ounces boiled ham (turkey ham is fine, too), cut into ¼-inch dice

About ⅔ cup fresh peas, blanched, or frozen peas, defrosted

½ cup cottage cheese

2 ounces feta cheese or blue cheese, crumbled

1 cup shredded Gruyère, Appenzeller, Comté, or Emmenthal cheese

¼ cup freshly grated Parmesan or pecorino

14 to 16 ounces small rigatoni or another fairly wide tubular pasta

HOT AND SPICY MAC AND CHEESE
WITH SALSA, MUSTARD, AND GREEN CHILES

Serves
4

This Southwestern riff on mac and cheese is rich in oozing cheese, tangy mustard, and enough hot chile to wake you up and make you take notice. If you don't want to bake this, serve it as soon as you have tossed it all together. Either way, you'll love it!

Sometimes I serve pickled jalapeños with this, either sliced and tossed into the pot or served whole alongside. Grilled spicy sausages such as Yucatecan, red chile, or spicy smoked duck are rather delicious alongside. Accompany with a salad of leafy greens tossed with olive oil and fresh lemon juice.

3 tablespoons unsalted butter

1 tablespoon flour

1 cup hot, but not boiling, milk (low-fat is fine)

1 roasted, peeled, and chopped Anaheim chile (see page 63), or 1 small (4.5 ounces) can diced mild green chiles

1 tablespoon medium salsa, homemade or good-quality store-bought

¼ teaspoon ground cumin

2 tablespoons sour cream (low-fat is fine)

1 to 2 teaspoons Dijon mustard

3 cloves garlic, chopped

½ to 1 teaspoon paprika

2½ cups shredded sharp Cheddar cheese

12 ounces small shell-shaped pasta

Salt and freshly ground black pepper to taste

Preheat the oven to 375°F. Bring a large pot of salted water to a boil.

In a heavy nonstick saucepan melt 1½ tablespoons of the butter over medium-low heat, then sprinkle in the flour. Cook for a minute or two. Remove from the heat and add the hot milk all at once, stirring with a wooden spoon. Return to the stove and, over a medium-high heat, cook the mixture, stirring constantly, until it thickens, about 5 to 7 minutes. If any lumps remain, whisk the sauce with a wire whisk for a few moments. If a few lumps remain, do not worry as no one will notice them when they are combined with the pasta and cheese. Add the green chile, salsa, cumin, sour cream, mustard, garlic, paprika, and 2 cups of the cheese. Stir to mix and set the sauce aside.

Cook the pasta in a large pot of rapidly boiling salted water until almost al dente and drain. Toss the hot pasta with the sauce, season with salt and pepper, then pour the mixture into a buttered 1½- to 2-quart baking dish with 4-inch sides. Sprinkle the remaining ½ cup of cheese on top, and dot with the remaining 1½ tablespoons of butter.

Bake the casserole until bubbly and the top is lightly browned in places, 15 to 20 minutes. Serve hot.

SOUFFLÉED ONIONY MACARONI AND CHEESE

Serves
4

Mmmm, this is the sort of dish to eat after a day of skiing, or even yodeling. Its flavor is essentially Alpine, though Italian Alpine, inspired by a totally Baroque wedding feast dish from Italy's northern borders: a roasted whole porchetta stuffed with macaroni and cheese.

I've found that the best accompaniment to this delicate macaroni and cheese is roast pork with a lovely jus of defatted pan juices and just enough broth to make a thin, well-flavored sauce. If you aren't roasting pork today, then chops work equally well. And if neither is on the horizon, or you are kosher, halal, or a vegetarian, make a simple little pan sauce by lightly browning several sliced garlic cloves in a teaspoon or two of olive oil along with a pinch of dried herbs, adding a cup of broth (chicken, beef, or vegetable), and cooking it down to about half its volume. Add a few drops of lemon juice and you have a lovely jus to serve alongside the rich macaroni.

The oniony sweetness of this dish and delicacy of the cheese call for a little salad of vinaigrette-dressed mâche alongside to refresh in between rich, cheesy bites.

Preheat the oven to 400°F.

In a small frying pan melt 2 tablespoons of the butter and lightly sauté the onion over medium heat until softened. Add half the wine and cook until the liquid is absorbed; continue stirring and cook for a few minutes longer, until the onion is golden. Sprinkle in the flour and cook for a minute or two, until the flour's rawness is gone. Remove from the heat and add the milk all at once, stirring with a wooden spoon. Return to the heat and cook, stirring, until the mixture is thickened, about 5 to 7 minutes. Whisk with a wire whisk for a few moments if any lumps remain. Season with salt, cayenne, and nutmeg. Add the remaining 1½ tablespoons of wine and remove from the heat. Stir in the crème fraîche, and three-fourths of the cheese; stir well and set aside.

cont'd

3 tablespoons unsalted butter

1 large onion, chopped

3 tablespoons dry white wine

1 tablespoon flour

1 cup hot, but not boiling, milk (low-fat is fine)

Salt to taste

A few grains of cayenne pepper

A grating of fresh nutmeg

½ cup crème fraîche or sour cream

cont'd.

8 ounces Emmenthaler, Appenzeller, Berkase, Gruyère, or graviera, shredded

6 ounces macaroni

3 egg whites

3 tablespoons chopped fresh chives

Cook the pasta in a large pot of rapidly boiling salted water until almost al dente and drain. Toss the macaroni with the sauce.

Whip the egg whites with a pinch of salt until soft peaks form.

Fold about a third of the whipped egg whites into the macaroni and sauce mixture to lighten it, and then fold in the rest. Butter a 1½- to 2-quart baking dish with the remaining 1 tablespoon of butter, then gently tip the pasta and cheese mixture into the dish. Sprinkle the top with the remaining cheese.

Bake for about 25 minutes, or until the top has puffed a bit and is browned in spots. Serve immediately, sprinkled with chives and surrounded with a bit of the pan sauce or jus as described in the headnote, or simply on its ow n.

CAJUN MACARONI AND CHEESE

In the bayou, no picnic, potluck, Thanksgiving, or Christmas is complete without a big pan of macaroni and cheese. And truth to tell, it is usually a classic creamy and Cheddary one. However, inspired on a recent trip to the bayou by the hearty jambalayas, zesty pickles, mustards, spices, and hot sauces (such as the legendary Tabasco), I've been whipping up this macaroni and cheese.

Serves
4

Preheat oven to 375°F. Cook the pasta in a large pot of rapidly boiling salted water until almost al dente, and drain.

In a large, heavy-bottom saucepan lightly sauté the onion over medium heat in the olive oil until it softens, 5 to 7 minutes. Stir in the garlic, cook for a few moments to mellow, and sprinkle in the flour. Cook for a minute or two until its raw flavor is gone. Remove from the heat, and add the bay leaf and the milk all at once. Return to the heat and cook, stirring with a wooden spoon, for 5 to 10 minutes, or until the sauce thickens. If any floury lumps remain, whisk the sauce with a wire whisk for a few moments. Remove from heat and set aside.

Remove the bay leaf from the sauce. Combine the macaroni with the sauce, and mix in the diced bell pepper, mustard seeds, thyme, paprika, chili powder, prepared mustard, dry mustard, Cheddar cheese (reserving ¼ cup for the topping), sliced olives, salt and pepper, and hot sauce. Pour into a large, shallow baking pan. Sprinkle the top with the reserved cheese, then with the crumbs, and dot with butter.

Bake for 30 minutes, or until the topping is golden, the cheese melty, and the crumbs crispy. Serve right away.

12 ounces small elbows or shells

1 onion, chopped

2 tablespoons olive oil

1 clove garlic, chopped

2 tablespoons flour

1 bay leaf

1½ cups hot, but not boiling, milk

½ green bell pepper, diced

½ teaspoon mustard seeds

½ teaspoon fresh thyme leaves, or ¼ teaspoon dried thyme, crushed between your fingers

1 teaspoon paprika

1 teaspoon chili powder

1 teaspoon prepared yellow or Creole mustard

½ teaspoon dry mustard

12 ounces sharp Cheddar, shredded

15 to 20 pimiento-stuffed green olives, sliced

Salt and freshly ground black pepper to taste

A few shakes of hot sauce, such as Tabasco

3 tablespoons cracker crumbs or stale breadcrumbs

1 tablespoon unsalted butter

CLARK WOLF'S WACKY
MACARONI AND CHEESEBURGER

Serves
4

This dish is named after Clark Wolf, the legendary foodie consultant who knows everyone and everything happening on either coast and most of what's going on in between, especially if it has to do with fabulous restaurants or cheese. In fact, if anyone in America is milking animals and making cheese, Clark probably knows about him or her.

Clark is a macaroni and cheese devotee and recently he shared with me his newest creation. "You've gotta make it!" he exclaimed. And so I did. Use chewy cavateppi ("squiggles for adults" says Clark) and a good, strong Cheddar: Clark recommends an aged New York or Wisconsin, Ig Vella's raw milk from California, or a Grafton four-year-old from Vermont. To balance the rich cheese, use lean beef. Oh, you can top the creation with a strip of crisp bacon if you like—Clark is quite emphatic that you do—and I think a few slices of ripe tomatoes along with a dab of full-flavored mustard are good on the side.

The mac and cheese should be made a day ahead, so you can easily cut it from the pan and assemble the burgers.

3 tablespoons unsalted butter

1 medium onion, chopped

3 tablespoons dry white wine

1 tablespoon flour

1 cup hot, but not boiling, milk (low-fat is fine)

A grating of fresh nutmeg

Salt and freshly ground black or white
  pepper to taste

A few grains of cayenne pepper

½ cup crème fraiche or sour cream (low-fat
  is fine)

8 ounces very sharp mature Cheddar, shredded

2 tablespoons freshly grated Parmesan

Preheat the oven to 400°F.

In a small frying pan, melt 1½ tablespoons of the butter over medium-low heat. Lightly sauté the onion until softened, then add 1½ tablespoons of the wine and cook until the onion begins to soften and the liquid is absorbed. Continue to cook, stirring and encouraging the onion to turn golden and soft. Sprinkle in the flour and cook for a minute or two, until the flour's rawness is gone. Remove from the heat and add the milk all at once, stirring with a wooden spoon. Return to the heat and cook, stirring, for 5 to 7 minutes, or until the mixture is thickened. If any lumps remain, whisk the sauce for a few moments with a wire whisk. Season with nutmeg, salt and pepper, and cayenne. Add the remaining 1½ tablespoons of wine and remove from the stove.

6 ounces short round pasta, such as cavateppi, ditali, or elbow macaroni

2 egg whites

1½ pounds lean ground chuck or sirloin

1 shallot, minced

Stir in the crème fraîche and three-fourths of the Cheddar and Parmesan cheeses; stir well and set aside.

Cook the pasta in a large pot of rapidly boiling salted water until almost al dente and drain. Toss with the sauce.

Whip the egg whites with a pinch of salt until soft peaks form. Fold a third of the whipped egg whites into the macaroni and sauce mixture to lighten it, then fold in the rest.

With the remaining 1½ tablespoons of butter, butter a large shallow baking pan. Gently pour the mixture in, and sprinkle the top with the remaining cheese.

Bake for about 25 minutes, or until the top has puffed a bit and is browned in spots. Leave to cool.

Using a round, open food mold (the kind that looks like a tin can open at both ends, which restaurants use to make perfect rounds of food on the plate), cut into the macaroni and cheese to make 4 rounds. An actual tin can, washed and dried, also works, and a sharp paring knife works well, too. If you can't manage a round, cut the macaroni and cheese into squares or triangles.

Combine lean beef with the shallot and form 4 thick patties about ¾ to 1 inch larger in diameter than the rounds of macaroni and cheese.

In a heavy nonstick frying pan, sear the patties on both sides, then place them on a baking sheet. Sear the bottoms of the macaroni and cheese rounds and place one on top of each patty.

Sprinkle some of the remaining Cheddar and Parmesan cheese on top of each macaroni-and-cheese-topped burger. Bake until the cheese melts and the meat is cooked to your liking (rare is really best for this), 5 to 7 minutes. Serve immediately.

GRATIN OF PENNE WITH ARTICHOKES AND FOUR CHEESES

Serves
4

Fresh artichokes are delish in this cheesy macaroni gratin, but the dish is so tasty that if fresh are not available, it is yummy even with frozen artichokes. And if they are not available, it is toothsome even with . . . yes, even with canned artichokes!

A mélange of different cheeses make the dish. I tend to throw it together with whatever small pieces I have on hand: something nutty and good for melting, such as a Comté, Emmenthal, or Gruyère; something slightly creamy, such as fontina; a pungent Stilton or Gorgonzola or a mild blue from France or Germany; and to finish it off, something hard and wonderful for grating. When I started making this dish, that last cheese was Parmesan, then I morphed through pecorino, and right now my favorite is halloumi cheese, grated on the fine grate of my cheese grater. It's salty and keeps its lovely character, lending a funkier nature to the gratin.

10 ounces penne, small rigatoni, or thin elbow macaroni (maccheroncini)

About 8 ounces cooked fresh artichoke hearts; frozen artichokes, defrosted; or canned (not marinated) artichokes, rinsed in cold water

3 to 4 cloves garlic, chopped

¼ cup crème fraîche

3 ounces fontina, shredded

4 ounces Emmenthal, Comté, or Gruyère, shredded

3 ounces Stilton cheese, crumbled

2 to 3 ounces halloumi, pecorino, or Parmesan cheese, grated

Salt and freshly ground black pepper to taste

Cook the pasta in a large pot of rapidly boiling salted water until almost al dente. Drain and transfer to a large shallow baking pan. Leave the pasta to cool so it's easier to toss and less likely to fall apart.

Preheat oven to 350°F. Dice the artichokes.

Toss the pasta with the artichokes, garlic, and crème fraîche. Toss in the fontina, Emmenthal, and Stilton, one by one. Before adding the halloumi, set aside 2 to 3 tablespoons. Season with salt and pepper and sprinkle the reserved halloumi over the top.

Bake for 20 to 25 minutes, or until the top is lightly browned and crisped in places and the cheese has melted. Serve immediately.

MACARRONES ALLA MALAGUENA

Mac and Cheese with Flamenco Flavors

Serves
4

The zesty flavors in this dish are as colorfully delicious as a flamenco dance: red bell peppers, tomatoes, zucchini, chorizo, peas, green beans, and briny green olives. I even like to eat it the next day, cold from the pan, though of course, you could use a plate.

In Spain, chorizo is an entire food group. There are uncooked little spicy ones and gentler ones without the hot sting. And there are cured skinny and fat salami-like chorizo, ready to eat, sliced up, as a tapa or *bocadillo* (sandwich). The hard chorizos are also delicious cooked with pasta and vegetables, as in this dish. Rigatoni is a good choice here because the sauce and bits of chorizo, vegetables, and olives get caught in the fat, floppy tubes.

10 ounces medium to large rigatoni

¼ cup extra-virgin olive oil

5 cloves garlic, chopped

1 red bell pepper, cut into ¼-inch dice

1 zucchini, cut into ¼- to ½-inch dice

3 ounces hard Spanish chorizo, cut into ¼-inch strips

½ cup fresh peas, blanched, or frozen peas, defrosted

½ cup fresh green beans, or frozen green beans, defrosted

3 cups diced tomatoes, fresh or canned, with their juices

2 to 3 tablespoons tomato paste

Large pinch of oregano

16 to 20 pimiento-stuffed green olives, thinly sliced

Salt and freshly ground black pepper to taste

8 to 9 ounces manchego, medium Asiago, aged Gouda, or a youngish pecorino cheese, thinly sliced

Cook the pasta in a large pot of rapidly boiling salted water until almost al dente. Drain and reserve about ¼ cup of the cooking liquid. Set the pasta aside while you cook the sauce.

Preheat the oven to 375°F.

In a large, heavy nonstick frying pan, heat the olive oil over medium-low heat and lightly sauté the garlic, but don't let it brown. Add the bell pepper and zucchini, sauté lightly until both vegetables soften, and then add the chorizo, peas, and green beans and cook together for about 5 minutes. Add the tomatoes, tomato paste, and oregano, and cook for a few minutes, until you have a flavorful sauce. Remove from the heat and stir in the olives. Season with salt and pepper, and add more oregano if needed. Toss the pasta with the sauce.

Arrange the pasta and sauce in a layer in the bottom of a large, shallow baking pan. Layer the thinly sliced manchego on top. Bake for 10 to 15 minutes, or long enough to melt the cheese and heat the macaroni and vegetables through. Serve immediately.

MAMBO ITALIANO

An Eggplant Turban Filled with Pasta and Lots of Good Things!

Serves
4 to 6

This big, fat concoction—tasty browned eggplant slices wrapped around a filling of macaroni, sauce, and cheese, with nuggets of salami here and there—is so flamboyantly tasty that it makes me want to dance the mambo Italiano each time I prepare it. As the eggplant is wrapped around the filling, it forms a turbanlike shape. (When I e-mailed a friend and described my eggplant turban, she imagined me with a big eggplant wrapped around my head!)

While most pasta is best when freshly prepared, this is an exception: It's even better the second day. Make it a day ahead and reheat in the casserole dish in a 350°F oven. Or, if you eat the dish the day you prepare it, reheat the leftovers in a nonstick frying pan, broken up a bit so that the cheese browns in spots and the eggplant winds around the macaroni here and there. It's the ultimate comfort food!

Sprinkle the eggplant with salt and let sit for about 30 minutes to draw out the liquid. Rinse and pat dry.

Heat about 1 tablespoon of the olive oil over medium heat in a heavy nonstick frying pan and brown the eggplant slices lightly, in batches, without crowding, adding more oil as needed. As the slices are done, lay them all out on a baking sheet and set aside. If they seem oily, pat dry with a paper towel.

Cook the pasta in a large pot of rapidly boiling salted water until just barely al dente. Drain and set aside.

Preheat oven to 375°F.

cont'd

2 unpeeled eggplants, cut lengthwise into ⅛- to ¼-inch thick slices

Salt for sprinkling

¼ cup extra-virgin olive oil, or as needed

12 ounces tiny salad macaroni, ditalini, elbow macaroni (maccheroncini), or the small rings known as anellini

6 ounces sweet Italian sausage, cut up into bite-size pieces

1 onion, chopped

One 12-ounce can chopped tomatoes, with their juices

cont'd

3 tablespoons tomato paste

Small pinch of sugar

Salt and freshly ground black pepper to taste

½ teaspoon fennel seeds, or to taste

Large pinch of dried oregano

3 to 4 ounces dry Italian salami, thinly sliced
and then cut into strips

8 to 10 ounces ricotta cheese

6 ounces mozzarella cheese, cut into
bite-size pieces

3 ounces Parmesan cheese, grated

In a clean large frying pan over medium heat, brown the sausage pieces. Remove from the pan and set aside. Pour off any fat in the pan. Add a tablespoon of the oil, then add the onion and lightly sauté until the onion is softened, 5 to 6 minutes. Add the chopped tomatoes and juice, stir for a few moments, then add the tomato paste, sugar, salt and pepper, fennel seeds, and oregano. Remove from the heat and set aside.

Line a 3-quart soufflé or deep round baking dish with the eggplant slices. Arrange the slices vertically, so the ends form a sunburst pattern on the bottom. Add a second, vertical layer. The upper edge of each slice will hang over the edge of the pan. You will use these floppy ends to close up the pasta casserole. There will be a few leftover slices for the top.

Combine the sauce with the cooked and drained pasta. Layer a third of this on the bottom of the eggplant-lined pan. Pat it down, then layer half the sausage, half the salami, half the ricotta in big dollops, half the mozzarella, and half the Parmesan. Repeat the layers. Top with the rest of the pasta in an even layer, and pat down firmly. Fold the eggplant slices overhanging the dish over the top of the pasta, and place the remaining eggplant on top of that.

Cover the casserole tightly with a lid or foil. Bake for about 30 minutes, or until heated through completely.

Cut into the casserole and serve.

ALLEN LAIDLOW'S TRINIDADIAN MACARONI PIE

Serves
4 to 6

Recently, as I was waiting in line to eat over-easy eggs and creamy grits at *The New York Times* commissary, I mulled over a friend's obsession with macaroni pie, the spicy macaroni and cheese dish so beloved throughout the Caribbean islands that were once part of the British Empire. My friend had been enthusiastically eating macaroni pie in Barbados, in true Bajan style: cut into slabs as a side dish for fried fish. Now that she was home, she wanted me to get a good recipe for it.

Hearing the accents in line, I asked if anyone knew macaroni pie. "Ask the cook, Allen Laidlow, from Trinidad," suggested the man next to me. "He makes great macaroni pie!" And so, in between flipping eggs, turning pancakes, and browning potatoes, Chef Laidlow described how he makes his macaroni pie, adding this admonition: "Its gotta be spicy—I use a lot of black pepper! Lots of black pepper!"

Macaroni pie is not, as might be assumed, a crust filled with macaroni (though in Italy there are such concoctions, many delicious). A Caribbean macaroni pie is simply macaroni and cheese, very thick, solidified by the addition of eggs and the right balance of pasta, sauce, and cheese. In fact, it is so solid that it's eaten cut into pieces rather than spooned up. This recipe is based loosely on Chef Allen's description, though I added manchego cheese to the Cheddar, and a big hit of hot pepper sauce, even though Laidlow says he doesn't use it. The abundance of black pepper gives a warm fragrance to the dish as well as a spicy kick. I varied the pepper kick by using a combination of mixed peppercorns and black. If you don't want to darken your macaroni pie with the black peppercorns, use white pepper instead. Leftovers are divine. I had mine for breakfast! If you mix the sizes of macaroni, as I did—small elbows and larger, fatter, penne—you will enhance the texture of the macaroni pie when eaten cold. It will be nice and firm where the small macaroni are, lightened with airy spaces where you find the larger penne. You could, of course, use only one type of pasta.

2 tablespoons unsalted butter or olive oil

1 onion, finely chopped

2 tablespoons flour

1½ cups hot, but not boiling, milk (low-fat is fine)

Preheat the oven to 375°F.

In a heavy nonstick saucepan over medium heat, melt the butter or heat the olive oil and lightly sauté the onion until it softens and turns slightly golden. Sprinkle with the flour and cook for few moments until the raw taste of the flour is gone. Remove from the heat and add the milk all

3 to 4 ounces penne

5 ounces small elbow macaroni

3 tablespoons sour cream (low-fat is fine) or crème fraîche

8 ounces sharp Cheddar, shredded

4 ounces manchego cheese, shredded

1 teaspoon freshly ground mixed peppercorns

1 teaspoon freshly ground black pepper

⅛ teaspoon freshly grated nutmeg

2 green onions (white and tender green parts), thinly sliced

Salt to taste

2 eggs, lightly beaten

Several generous shakes of hot sauce, such as Tabasco or a Caribbean hot sauce, or to taste

at once, stirring with a wooden spoon. Return to the heat and cook, stirring, for 5 to 7 minutes, or until the sauce is thickened. If there are floury lumps, whisk with a wire whisk. Set the sauce aside.

Cook the penne in a large pot of rapidly boiling salted water until halfway to al dente, then add the elbow macaroni and continue to cook until both pastas are almost al dente, and drain.

Combine the drained pastas with the sour cream, sauce, Cheddar and manchego cheeses (except for 2 to 3 tablespoons of each to reserve for the topping), mixed peppercorns, black pepper, nutmeg, green onions, salt, beaten eggs, and hot sauce.

Pour out into a large shallow baking pan, and sprinkle with the reserved Cheddar and manchego. Bake for 25 to 35 minutes, or until the top is melty and golden brown in spots. Eat right away hot, or better yet, eat the next day, cold, Caribbean style.

Macaroni Pie with Curry Spice: Squares of cold macaroni pie with a little sprinkle of curry powder to dip them in is my own personal pleasure. Sometimes I add a scattering of cilantro, too. Use a good-quality curry powder and sprinkle it on the plate around your portion, or on top if you prefer, and scatter sprigs of cilantro wherever you wish. The combination of curry and cheese is not as culinarily far-fetched as it sounds. When many Caribbean islands were part of the British Empire, workers were brought to the region from India, and with them, their spices.

MACARONIS AU GRATIN VA VA VA VOOM

Serves
4

This creamy macaroni and cheese topped with roasted mushrooms is so French in flavor, I can't help saying Va Va Va Voom! Gruyère is delicious in this dish, especially a really good cave-aged Gruyère. Other excellent cheeses from Switzerland, France, or Germany, such as Appenzeller, Emmenthal, Comté, fontina, or Berkase, are luscious in the creamy, tender macaroni. As soothing as the macaroni and cheese mixture is, however, the focus of this dish is its topping of mushrooms dotted with butter. As they roast, the dabs of butter melt into the mushroom juices and the hit of garlic, making a lovely, deep jus that seeps into the macaroni and cheese they rest on. The mushrooms keep their character, and when you bite in, and the juices hit the macaroni and cheese, something wonderful happens in your mouth! You can use this technique of roasting mushrooms on top of macaroni with a leftover dish of a delicate nature, such as the Macaroni and Double Asparagus Gratin (facing page).

12 ounces small macaroni, such as elbows or pennette

4 cloves garlic, chopped

1 shallot, chopped

10 to 12 ounces Gruyère, Appenzeller, Emmenthal, Comté, or Berkase cheese, shredded

4 ounces crème fraîche, or as desired

A grating of fresh nutmeg

Salt and freshly ground black pepper to taste

5 tablespoons unsalted butter

8 to 12 ounces medium mushrooms, stems removed

1 tablespoon chopped fresh chives

1 tablespoon chopped chervil or parsley

1 to 2 teaspoons pink peppercorns (optional)

Preheat oven to 375°F. Cook the pasta in a large pot of rapidly boiling salted water until it is barely al dente. Drain, and reserve about 1 cup of the cooking liquid.

Return the hot pasta to the pan immediately, and toss with about a quarter of the garlic, all of the shallot, half the shredded cheese (sprinkled evenly over the top), the crème fraîche, nutmeg, salt and pepper, and 2 tablespoons of the butter. Ladle in about ¼ cup of the cooking liquid and toss again. Then add the remaining cheese and toss one more time.

Spoon the mixture into a large shallow baking pan and lay the mushroom caps, smooth side down and open side up, on top of the macaroni and cheese mixture. Dab the mushrooms with as much of the remaining 3 tablespoons of butter you can squeeze into the caps. Sprinkle with the remaining garlic and season with salt and pepper.

Bake for 20 to 25 minutes, or long enough for the mushrooms to brown lightly, and delicious juices to accumulate in the cups of the mushrooms.

Sprinkle with the chives and chervil and the pink peppercorns, if desired, and eat right away. Serve each person a mushroom or two along with a portion of the macaroni and cheese from below.

MACARONI AND DOUBLE ASPARAGUS GRATIN

Serves
4

Here the layer of pasta is tossed with pureed asparagus, butter, and a little shredded cheese; then it's topped with béchamel, asparagus tips, and a flurry of shredded cheese. The whole thing bakes into a casserole with a rich, soothing topping lightly crisped around the edges. Underneath, the pasta is bathed in the essence of asparagus. Any leftovers can be reheated in the oven, or transformed into the mushroom-topped Macaronis au Gratin Va Va Va Voom (facing page). Just add the mushroom topping and heat it together, as directed in that recipe.

Trim only the very dry, very tough edges off the stems of the asparagus instead of snapping them as usual. Cut off each tender tip with some of the stem, so that it is about 4 to 5 inches long. Cut the remaining stems crosswise into ¼- to ½-inch slices.

In a heavy large saucepan, heat the 1 cup of water until boiling and season with salt. Add the asparagus tips and cook over high heat for almost 1 minute, or long enough to blanch. Remove from the hot water with tongs, and leave the asparagus tips to cool until you are ready to use them for the topping. Add the sliced asparagus stems to the hot cooking water and cook for about 2 minutes. Drain, reserving about ¾ cup of the cooking liquid. Season with salt and pepper and set aside.

Puree the sliced asparagus in a food processor with the garlic and enough of the reserved cooking water to make a thick sauce, rather than a chunky paste. Add 3 tablespoons of the butter to the pureed asparagus mixture and set aside.

cont'd

1 bunch asparagus

1 cup water

Salt and freshly ground black pepper to taste

1 to 2 cloves garlic, chopped

6 tablespoons unsalted butter, or as needed

12 ounces elbow macaroni or small shells

3 tablespoons flour

2 cups hot, but not boiling, milk (low-fat is fine)

A few grains of cayenne pepper, or to taste

A grating of fresh nutmeg

8 ounces Appenzeller, Gruyère, Emmenthal, Comté, or Greek graviera cheese, shredded

2 tablespoons freshly grated Parmesan, or as desired

cont'd

Preheat the oven to 375°F. Cook the pasta in a large pot of rapidly boiling salted water until barely al dente. Drain and set aside.

In a heavy nonstick saucepan, heat 2 tablespoons of the butter over medium-low heat, then sprinkle in the flour. Cook for a minute or two or until the raw taste of the flour is gone. Remove from the heat and add the milk at once, stirring with a wooden spoon. Return to the stove, and over medium-high heat, cook the mixture, stirring constantly, until thickened. Season with salt, cayenne, and nutmeg. Set aside to thicken as it cools; this should take about 30 minutes. If it is too warm, it will sink too far down into the pasta, rather than remaining near the top.

In a large bowl, combine the cooked pasta with the pureed asparagus mixture and mix in half the Appenzeller cheese. Then layer this in the bottom of a large shallow baking pan. Spoon the béchamel sauce over the top. Do not worry if it sits on top of the pasta in blobs and dabs; don't try to smooth it down, as it will mix with the pasta if you do. Sprinkle with the remaining Appenzeller cheese, arrange the asparagus tips on the top in an appealing pattern, and sprinkle the top with the Parmesan. Dot with the remaining 1 tablespoon of butter.

Bake for about 20 minutes, or until the top is lightly browned in spots and the whole casserole is sizzling. Serve right away.

NOODLES AND CHEESE FROM A TURKISH VILLAGE

Serves
4

One summer I found myself on a nearly empty shore of Antalya, Turkey, for several weeks of vacation. I knew it would be nice, but was unprepared for how magical and marvelous it was. We swam in cool, clear salty water when the days were sweltering and drank endless glasses of sweet tea with the villagers. And nearly every day we ate sweet, juicy watermelon purchased from a truck that drove through the village each afternoon around four.

One day the mayor's wife made lunch: sweet, ripe tomato salad, roasted peppers, garlicky spinach mixed with yogurt, and something very much like this dish of noodles and cheese.

10 ounces fresh egg lasagne sheets or wide egg noodles, or 8 ounces dried lasagne or wide noodles

3 to 4 tablespoons unsalted butter

6½ to 7 ounces Turkish white cheese, such as beyaz peynir, or feta cheese, preferably Bulgarian, Greek, or Israeli

6½ to 7 ounces cottage cheese

8 ounces bland fresh white cheese, such as quark, fromage frais, or farmers' cheese (or omit, and double the amount of cottage cheese)

3 to 4 green onions (white and green parts), thinly sliced

2 to 3 tablespoons chopped fresh cilantro

2 to 3 tablespoons chopped fresh dill

2 eggs, lightly beaten

2 to 3 tablespoons sour cream (low-fat is fine), Greek yogurt, or laban (strained Middle Eastern yogurt cheese)

Salt and freshly ground black pepper to taste

4 to 6 ounces firm Turkish cheese, such as kasar peynir, Greek kasseri, or a mild white Cheddar or Jack, shredded

Preheat the oven to 350°F.

Cook the lasagne noodles in a large pot of rapidly boiling generously salted water until barely al dente. (Since lasagne noodles are so large and you will need about 8 or so, you can boil them one at a time.) Remove from the hot water and dunk immediately into a pan of cold water to cool. Remove from the cold water and place on a piece of plastic wrap while you finish cooking the rest. This way, they won't stick to each other.

Generously butter the inside of a large shallow baking pan or lasagne pan and dot about 1 tablespoon of butter around the bottom. Layer 1 or 2 sheets of lasagne noodles in the pan and dot with a little more butter. Mix the Turkish cheese, cottage cheese, and quark together. In layers, add a quarter of the cheese mixture, sprinkled with a third of the green onions, cilantro, and dill. Beat the eggs together with the sour cream and the salt and pepper and spoon about a third of this over the cheese mixture then sprinkle with a quarter of the shredded Turkish cheese. Repeat the layers 2 more times, beginning with the lasagne. Finally, add the remaining cheese mixture, the remaining shredded cheese, and dot the dish with the remaining butter.

Bake for 25 to 30 minutes, or until the edges of the lasagne are lightly crisped and brown, and the cheese is bubbly and browned in spots.

Let sit for a few minute to settle, and then serve hot.

PASTITSIO

Greek Macaroni with Meat Sauce and Cheesy Béchamel

Serves
4 to 6

When I lived in Greece, whenever I visited the local taverna and was invited back into the kitchen to see what was being served, I always looked at the moussaka, and then the pastitsio, and then the moussaka again, trying to decide which one looked best. I'm a glutton when it comes to eggplant, however, so I always ended up with the moussaka, and would end up gazing longingly at the pastitsio that one of my friends would inevitably order. Luckily, pastitsio is simple to prepare, and this is the classic: a layer of spiced meat sauce, a layer of macaroni, and a layer of cheesy custard on top. Baked just long enough for the top to puff and crisp in places, it is irresistible. And if you are craving eggplant—sometimes I do—simply add a layer of pan-browned eggplant slices in the bottom of the baking pan, underneath the meaty tomato sauce.

Start your meal with a little meze: a plate of olives, slices of cucumber, a little tzaziki (garlicky yogurt), some hummus mixed with finely chopped roasted red bell peppers, some steamed zucchini slices drizzled with olive oil and lemon, and glasses of a sleek Greek red.

Brown the beef and onion in a large nonstick frying pan over medium heat until it is broken up and lightly browned in spots. Add the wine and cook down until only a few spoonfuls of liquid remain. Add the broth, tomato paste, sugar, bay leaf, cinnamon, allspice, oregano, and salt and pepper. Bring to a boil and cook down until the mixture is saucy and strongly, deliciously flavored. Set aside.

Preheat the oven to 350°F.

Cook the pasta in a large pot of rapidly boiling salted water until barely al dente. Drain and set aside.

cont'd

12 ounces ground beef

½ onion, chopped

¾ cup red wine

1 cup beef broth, homemade or canned

3 heaping tablespoons tomato paste

Pinch of sugar, or to taste

1 bay leaf

½ teaspoon cinnamon, or to taste

Pinch of allspice

Large pinch of dried oregano leaves, crumbled between the fingers

Salt and freshly ground black pepper to taste

cont'd

12 ounces elbow macaroni, rigatoni, or another medium-size tubular pasta

3 tablespoons unsalted butter, or a combination of butter and olive oil

3 tablespoons flour

2½ cups hot, but not boiling, milk (low-fat is fine)

A grating of fresh nutmeg

Dash of cayenne pepper, or to taste

8 ounces kefalotyri, kasseri, graviera, or a combination of Greek cheeses, shredded (or substitute Cheddar, Ossau-Iraty Brebis, a mixture of Jack and dry Jack, or pecorino)

2 eggs, lightly beaten

In a heavy nonstick saucepan melt the butter over medium-low heat. Sprinkle with the flour and cook for a moment or two, until the raw taste of the flour is gone. Remove from the heat. Pour in the milk all at once, stirring well with a wooden spoon. Cook over medium-high heat, stirring, until the milk thickens nicely. If it is lumpy, whisk with a wire whisk for a few moments. Season with salt, pepper, nutmeg, and cayenne. Stir in two-thirds of the shredded cheese in several batches, stirring after each addition. Beat a few tablespoons of the sauce into the eggs to keep them from curdling when added to the saucepan. Repeat, and then add this creamy egg mixture to the rest of the sauce in the pan and mix well with the wooden spoon so that it becomes creamy and the eggs do not scramble.

Remove the bay leaf from meaty sauce and discard. Pour the meaty sauce into the bottom of a large shallow baking pan. Top with the macaroni in an even layer. Top the macaroni with the cheesy sauce, then sprinkle the remaining cheese over the top.

Bake for about 25 minutes, or until the top is slightly puffy and spotted on top with golden brown splotches. Serve immediately.

TRUFFLED TIMBALES WITH ZUCCHINI PESTO

Serves
6

Nubbins of small pasta, bound together in a creamy custard-like timbale, then served surrounded by zucchini and pesto: It's elegant, it's soothing and rich, and it just makes me happy to eat it!

Cook the pasta in a large pot of rapidly boiling salted water until almost al dente. Drain and set aside.

Heat the half-and-half in a small saucepan until it just begins to boil; slowly stir in the Gruyère and 2 ounces of the Parmesan cheese, in about 4 or 5 batches, stirring until each batch melts before adding more. Season with salt, cayenne pepper, and nutmeg and remove from the stove. In a large bowl, beat the eggs lightly. Pour a few spoonfuls of the cheese sauce into the eggs and mix well. Add the rest of the sauce and stir well again. Toss in the pasta, but don't stir; this will break apart the pasta. Just fold it in as if you were folding a soufflé.

Preheat the oven to 350°F.

Generously butter 6 timbale or individual soufflé dishes (¾ cup each) and divide the mixture evenly among them. Gently press down on the mixture to flatten it.

cont'd

4 ounces very thin elbow macaroni (maccheroncini)

10 ounces half-and-half

4 ounces Gruyère, Emmenthal, Appenzeller, Comté, or a similar cheese, shredded

2 ounces Parmesan cheese, grated, plus 2 to 3 tablespoons for the pesto

Salt to taste

Dash of cayenne pepper

A grating of fresh nutmeg

3 eggs

1 medium-large zucchini, diced

1 clove garlic

¼ cup coarsely torn or chopped fresh basil

3 to 4 tablespoons extra-virgin olive oil

Truffle oil for serving

Place the timbales in a baking pan and pour in boiling water to come about three-quarters of the way up. Place in oven and bake for 25 to 30 minutes, or until the tops are no longer jiggly. Remove from the oven and, with oven mitts, take the tambales out of the water bath.

While the timbales are baking, cook the zucchini in rapidly boiling salted water until tender. Drain well.

Put the garlic in a large mortar, add a pinch of salt, and crush with the pestle. Then work in the basil and olive oil. Put down the pestle and, using a spoon, stir in the remaining 2 to 3 tablespoons of Parmesan cheese and then the cooked zucchini.

Run a knife around the inner edge of each timbale. Place a plate on top and invert the timbale. Give the bottom of the dish a strong tap, then gently remove it. It should come off easily. If not, you can always tidy it up a bit with your spoon.

Shake a few drops of truffle oil on and around each timbale, then spoon a little of the pesto-zucchini mixture around as well. Serve immediately.

Truffled Turkey Tetrazzini: The day after Thanksgiving, when you've regained your appetite, alternate layers of leftover turkey with the macaroni mixture for the timbales. Sprinkle the top with grated Gruyère and Parmesan, and bake as instructed. Instead of zucchini pesto, enjoy a more wintery accompaniment of sautéed sliced or diced mushrooms—so delicious with truffle, turkey, and pasta!

MACARONI AND CHEESE FRITTATA
WITH SALAMI, GREENS, AND ZUCCHINI

I ate this on a hillside vineyard overlooking the Bay of Naples, under a pergola of hanging grapes and a lattice of vines. As night fell we could see through the vines to the stars in the black sky.

Along with this frittata, we ate bread splashed with olive oil and topped with tomatoes and roasted peppers, and to follow, a big pot of stewed heirloom chickpeas and a crisp salad. Dessert was granita of almond syrup over crushed ice.

The pasta in our frittata was in fact, spaghetti, but I find small elbows make a more tender presentation. This dish is an example of *cucina povera*, "food of the poor." It's designed for using leftover pasta, but I like it so much that I often cook up pasta specially for the frittata. You'll need a large ovenproof nonstick sauté pan or frying pan.

This is terrific hot, but it's also good at cool room temperature on the antipasto table or for a picnic.

5 to 6 ounces small, thin elbow macaroni (maccheroncini)

3 ounces spicy salami, such as coppa or a red chile–seasoned salami from Calabria

1 zucchini, cut into ½-inch dice

3 cloves garlic, thinly sliced

3 tablespoons extra-virgin olive oil

Two handfuls (about 2 ounces) baby greens, such as beet greens, young chard, or spinach

6 eggs, lightly beaten

Preheat the oven to 400°F.

Cook the pasta in a large pot of rapidly boiling salted water until just tender; this will only take 4 to 5 minutes, as the macaroni are small. Drain and set aside.

In a large nonstick frying pan, lightly brown the salami over medium heat for about 4 minutes. Push it over to one side and add the zucchini, garlic, and 1 tablespoon of the olive oil. Cook for about 5 minutes, or until the zucchini has softened. Add the baby greens, toss thoroughly with the hot zucchini and salami, and cover. Cook for a few minutes, remove from the heat, and let cool slightly.

In a large bowl combine the beaten eggs with the macaroni and add the cheese. With a slotted spoon, transfer the salami and greens to the macaroni mixture (discard the juices from the vegetables or reserve them for another use such as soup), then season with salt, pepper, and thyme.

6 ounces kefalotyri or pecorino cheese, cut into ⅛- to ¼-inch dice

Salt and freshly ground black pepper to taste

Two big pinches of dried thyme leaves, crushed between the fingers

Heat the remaining 2 tablespoons of olive oil in a large, heavy ovenproof sauté or frying pan until it is smoking, then spoon in the frittata mixture. Reduce the heat to low, and smooth the top of the mixture so that it is even. Cook for 3 to 5 minutes, or until the bottom begins to cook and the egg binding the mixture begins to firm up.

Put the frittata in the oven and bake for 15 to 20 minutes, or until it feels relatively firm when touched lightly. You don't want this to be runny at all, though you do want it to remain moist.

Remove from oven and let sit 5 minutes or so. You can either serve it from the pan, cut into wedges as if it were a pie, or invert it onto a plate and then cut it.

To invert, loosen the edges with a cake spatula or knife, working it under the frittata if possible. Place a plate on top of the pan, then quickly invert them. Give a tap or two on the bottom of the pan. Hopefully, as you pull the pan away, you will be left with a golden brown pancake of pasta.

MACARONI AND CHEESE "BROCCOLISSIMO"

This dish is as much about the broccoli as it is about the macaroni. They are held together with lots of creamy béchamel, and baked into a melty pungent, delectable mess. Though I like it with Sprinz, a dry Jack, pecorino, or aged Asiago would be good here. Or use a combination of two cheeses, one mild, such as Jack, and one strong, such as pecorino.

For a refreshing and simple salad, serve slices of ripe tomatoes topped with leaves of Asian or anise basil. Either will push the edge of tomato and basil that little intriguing bit further.

Blanch the broccoli in a small amount of rapidly boiling salted water or steam them. Drain and set aside.

Cook the pasta in a large pot of rapidly boiling salted water until almost al dente, then drain and set aside.

In a heavy nonstick saucepan, melt the butter over medium-low heat, then sprinkle in the flour. Cook for a minute or so to get rid of the raw taste of the flour. Remove from the heat and add the milk all at once, stirring well with a wooden spoon. Return to the stove and cook, stirring, over medium-high heat until the sauce thickens. If there are any lumps, whisk them away with a wire whisk. Season with the salt, cayenne, and nutmeg. Set aside a few table-spoons of the cheese for the top of the casserole, and stir the rest into the sauce.

Spoon a few tablespoons of the sauce on the bottom of a large shallow baking dish, then in layers, add the pasta, broccoli, and the remaining sauce. Sprinkle the reserved cheese over the top.

Bake until the top is bubbling and hot, and the cheese melty and browning in spots, about 20 minutes. Serve immediately.

Serves
4

1 to 2 heads broccoli, stems cut into bite-size pieces, tops cut into small, bite-size florets

8 ounces small shell pasta

2 tablespoons unsalted butter

2 tablespoons flour

2 cups hot, but not boiling, milk (low-fat is fine)

Salt to taste

Dash of cayenne pepper

A grating of fresh nutmeg

10 ounces Sprinz or Asiago, shredded (or combination of 8 ounces Appenzeller, Jack, or a similar tasty firm cheese, shredded, plus 2 ounces pecorino, aged Asiago, or Parmesan, grated)

Macaroni and cheese for dessert? Have we gone too far?

In fact, tender pasta, sweetened and mixed with delicate cheeses, makes a few of the world's most delectable traditional desserts.

Our sweets go from a decidedly homey childhood favorite—*lokshen kugel* (page 125)— to the fragrant Lemon-Scented Pasta Pudding (page 127), which is so redolent of the Amalfi Coast you might feel like bursting into Italian. (At first bite, I always do). And then there is my own rendition of Falooda (page 123), an Indian sweet made with cornstarch noodles served with rosewater syrup and ice cream, to which I add a wonderfully refreshing ricotta cheese ice cream.

FALOODA

Falooda is a traditional Indian sweet of vermicelli—either wheat, rice, or the cornstarch ones made here—sweetened with syrup or coconut milk, and eaten with a scoop of rich ice cream. This was my inspiration, and it is a different sort of macaroni and cheese, indeed: squiggly noodles with a creamy, light ice cream made with ricotta cheese and Greek yogurt. A puddle of soaked dried cherries at the bottom of the bowl gilds the lily. It's a lyrical little dessert, and the most delicate, fragrant macaroni and cheese you could ever imagine!

I love everything about *falooda,* including the way it sounds, *fal-ooooooodah.* Even the word sounds yummy.

Make the noodles: In a medium nonstick saucepan, combine the cornstarch, sugar, and water and stir well. Cook over medium heat, stirring, until the mixture gets very thick, almost doughlike, about 5 to 8 minutes. Remove from the heat and stir in the rosewater. Let cool slightly, then pour onto a cutting board thickly dusted with cornstarch, and spread evenly. Cool completely.

With a chef's knife or cleaver, cut the dough into thin noodles 3 to 4 inches long, or longer if you desire (the dough can be a little clumsy to cut), and place the strips, which will now look a bit like noodles, into a bowl of iced water. Leave for 5 minutes or so, then remove and place on a plate. Cover with plastic wrap and chill until ready to use. You can make these ahead up to 3 days in advance and store in the refrigerator. When you're ready to serve, carefully pull them apart and, if necessary, recut.

Make the cherries: Combine all the ingredients in a cup or small bowl and stir well to dissolve the sugar. Let cool. You can prepare them up to 4 days in advance and store, covered, in the refrigerator.

cont'd

Serves
4

NOODLES

½ cup cornstarch, plus extra for dusting

2 tablespoons sugar

1¼ cups water

1 tablespoon rosewater

CHERRIES

½ cup boiling water

3 ounces dried Montmorency or Amarena cherries

5 tablespoons sugar

cont'd

**CARDAMON-SCENTED
RICOTTA-YOGURT ICE CREAM**

½ up sugar

1 cup water

8 ounces whole-milk ricotta

½ cup Greek yogurt (thick, whole milk
   yogurt), or regular whole milk yogurt

Seeds of 3 to 4 cardamom pods

Make the ice cream: In a small saucepan, combine the sugar and water. Bring to a boil and continue boiling for about 2 minutes, or until the sugar is totally dissolved and the liquid has become a thin, pale gold syrup. Remove from the heat and let cool to room temperature.

In a large metal bowl, stir the ricotta to smooth out the lumps. Then stir in the yogurt and whisk together until very smooth. Whisk in the syrup and beat until smooth. Whisk in the cardamom, transfer to an ice-cream maker and freeze according to the manufacturer's instructions. Or freeze in a metal bowl in your freezer. After about 45 minutes, stir and scrape down the sides of the bowl to keep the mixture smooth and return to the freezer. Repeat every 15 to 20 minutes thereafter. When the ice cream has frozen to a soft, lovely consistency it is ready. Transfer it to a plastic container if you are not using it right away so that it will stay supple for several hours; occasional stirring helps a great deal. If the mixture becomes icy hard, whirl it in the food processor to lighten and loosen, then serve.

To serve, spoon a little of the soaked cherries into each bowl and top with a scoop of ricotta ice cream. Garnish around the edges with the noodles, separating them if they have stuck together. Spoon more cherries and syrup over the noodles and around the ice cream. Eat right away.

DR. ESTHER'S LOKSHEN KUGEL WITH APPLE, GOLDEN RAISINS, AND COTTAGE CHEESE

Serves
4

Kugel is a pudding, a baked mixture of vegetables, fruit, or noodles. It can be savory, such as a potato kugel, savory and sweet such as the peppery caramelized Jerusalem noodle kugel, or as sweet and succulent as this one.

Dr. Esther is my longtime friend, and her late father was, without a doubt, the kugel king. When he fled Lithuania for the green pastures of Nebraska, he brought with him his old-country kugel-making skills. I was hooked the first time I took a bite: It was fragrant with cinnamon, rich with butter, and moist from the cottage cheese and grated apples. We bonded over this kugel, arguably the best in kugeldom.

Cook the pasta in a large pot of rapidly boiling salted water until just tender, then drain and return to the pot.

Preheat the oven to 350°F.

Melt the butter in a small saucepan. Add the melted butter and the remaining ingredients to the noodles and toss gently to combine.

Pour into a large shallow baking pan and bake for about 1 to 1½ hours, or until the top is crusty and brown. Eat hot or cold.

12 ounces wide flat noodles, preferably egg noodles

8 to 10 tablespoons unsalted butter

8 to 12 ounces cottage cheese

3 eggs, lightly beaten

2 apples, unpeeled, coarsely shredded

2 teaspoons ground cinnamon

1 cup sugar

½ cup golden raisins

½ teaspoon baking soda

LEMON-SCENTED PASTA PUDDING

This is a lot like a kugel, in that it is a sweet baked pudding made of pasta, in this case tiny orzo. This recipe, however, is from a village near Italy's Amalfi coast where lemons grow abundantly. The combination of lemon and ricotta give the pudding a sweet-tart flavor.

Serves
4 to 6

Preheat the oven to 375°F.

Cook the pasta in a large pot of rapidly boiling salted water until al dente and drain. Toss with the butter and set aside.

In a medium bowl, combine the lemon zest with the lemon juice, ricotta cheese, yogurt, sugar, eggs, and baking soda. Spoon into a large shallow baking dish.

Bake for about 30 minutes, or until the top is lightly browned and caramelized in spots and the pudding is no longer wobbly, but is not completely firm; you want it to keep a soft, yielding, texture.

Eat hot or at cool room temperature.

8 ounces orzo or another small rice-shaped pasta

4 to 6 tablespoons butter, melted

Grated zest of 2 organic lemons

Juice of 1 lemon

2 cups ricotta cheese

3 to 4 tablespoons Greek yogurt or sour cream

1 to 1¼ cups sugar

3 eggs, lightly beaten

¼ teaspoon baking soda

SOURCES FOR CHEESES

ARTISANAL CHEESE CENTER
500 West 37th Street
New York, NY 10018
TEL: (877) 797-1200
Eat at the restaurant, buy at the shop, study at the cheese center, or hire their function room for a party! A cheesy time awaits you.

ARTISAN CHEESE
2413 California Street
San Francisco, CA 94115
TEL: (415) 929-8610

BEDFORD CHEESE SHOP
218 Bedford Avenue
Brooklyn, NY 11211
TEL: (718) 599-7588
FAX: (718) 599-8644

THE CHEESEBOARD COLLECTIVE
1504 Shattuck Avenue
Berkeley, CA 94709
TEL: (510) 549-3183

COWGIRL CREAMERY
Tomales Bay Foods
80 Fourth Street
Point Reyes Station, CA 94956
TEL: (415) 663-9335
Artisan cheese from all over the world, including their own delectable hand-made cheeses. Look through the window and watch the cheesemakers in action!

COWGIRL CREAMERY CHEESE SHOP
San Francisco Ferry Plaza
1 Ferry Plaza, Unit 17
San Francisco, CA 94111
TEL: (415) 362-9350

COWGIRL CREAMERY
Mail Order and online ordering
TEL: (866) 433-7834 or
(707) 789-2604
www.cowgirlcreamery.com

MOUNT VIKOS ARTISANAL GREEK CHEESES
www.mount-vikos.com
Nationwide at finest cheese shops.

TRADER JOES
www.traderjoes.com
Stores across the United States with terrific cheeses—and pasta, too—all at a great price!

WHOLE FOODS
www.wholefoods.com
Stores across the United States with a good selection of cheeses.

ZINGERMAN'S
www.zingermans.com
At various locations in Ann Arbor, Michigan. Cheeses and other products can be ordered online.

In the United Kingdom

NEAL'S YARD DAIRY
6 Park Street
London, SE1 9AB United Kingdom
TEL: 020 7645 3558
FAX: 020 7645 3565
For a delightful romp through Britain's cheese.

INDEX

TABLE OF EQUIVALENTS

The exact equivalents in the following tables have been rounded for convenience.

LIQUID/DRY MEASURES

U.S.	Metric
¼ teaspoon	1.25 milliliters
½ teaspoon	2.5 milliliters
1 teaspoon	5 milliliters
1 tablespoon (3 teaspoons)	15 milliliters
1 fluid ounce (2 tablespoons)	30 milliliters
¼ cup	60 milliliters
⅓ cup	80 milliliters
½ cup	120 milliliters
1 cup	240 milliliters
1 pint (2 cups)	480 milliliters
1 quart (4 cups, 32 ounces)	960 milliliters
1 gallon (4 quarts)	3.84 liters
1 ounce (by weight)	28 grams
1 pound	454 grams
2.2 pounds	1 kilogram

LENGTH

U.S.	Metric
⅛ inch	3 millimeters
¼ inch	6 millimeters
½ inch	12 millimeters
1 inch	2.5 centimeters

OVEN TEMPERATURE

Fahrenheit	Celsius	Gas
250	120	½
275	140	1
300	150	2
325	160	3
350	180	4
375	190	5
400	200	6
425	220	7
450	230	8
475	240	9
500	260	10